Manual for Psy

Author: Mark Haden

With significant contributions by: Martin Ball PhD, Dr. Birgitta Woods, Lidija Martinovic, Bradley Foster, Dr. Devon Christie

Note to the reader

The information in this book should not be construed as advocating for the use of psychedelic substances outside of the context of legally sanctioned environments with appropriate supervision. Neither the author or the publisher assume any responsibility for any physical, psychological, legal or any other consequences from the use of these substances.

Kyandara Publishing
Ashland, Oregon
Vancouver, Canada

2020

Copyright 2020 by Mark Haden

All rights reserved. No part of this book may be reproduced or utilized in any form without permission in writing from the author.

We would like to thank the following people for making substantial contributions to this manual: Dr. Birgitta Woods
Martin Ball, Ph.D., Trina Nguyen, Lidija Rekert, Bradley Foster
Melania Lumezanu, Rick Minors, Dr. Devon Christie, Marcus Grail, Geffen Grail

We would also like to thank the following for their editorial support: Farhan Ahmed, Blake Rupert, Dr. Gordon Reid

Cover design and fractal images by Martin Ball, www.fractalimagination.com

Mark Haden

Table of Contents:

Forward i
Disclaimer 1
Preface – A Brief Summary of the Science 1
Choice of Language in This Manual 3
Introduction 5
Set and Setting 7
Space Issues 9
    Interview room 9
    Experience room 9
    Lighting 11
Ritualizing the Process 12
Presence and Intentions 15
Inner Healing Intelligence 17
The Role of the Guide 18
Qualities of Guides 18
    A Knowledgeable, Skilled and Wise Guide: 18
    Experiential Knowledge: 19
    Knowledge of the Human Mind When Seen Through the Lens of Psychedelics 19
    Knowledge of the Power and Importance of Human Relationships 20
    Appreciation of Human Suffering 21
The Skills of Being a Psychedelic Guide 23
    The Six Core Competencies 27
        1) Empathetic Abiding Presence 27
        2) Trust Enhancement 28
        3) Spiritual Intelligence 29
        4) Knowledge 29
        5) Self-Awareness and Ethical Integrity 30
        6) Proficiency in complementary techniques 30
Trauma Resolution skills 32
    What is Trauma? 32

Manual for Psychedelic Guides

Understanding the Origins of Trauma 32
Trauma is the "Ever Present Past" existing NOW, in the body 33
Trauma can be Spiritual 34
Physical Touch 34
Eye Contact 35
Body Language 35
Therapeutic Alliance 36
Should a Guide Take a Psychedelic at the Same Time as the Participant? 38
Should the Guide Have Personal Experiences with Psychedelics 38
Who Should Not Be a Psychedelic Guide? 39
Great Therapist Syndrome 39
Predator 40
Over-Bonding Problem 40
Trauma Projection 41
Initial Sessions 43
Red Flags 43
Green Flags 48
Challenging Situations as a Result of Poor Screening ... 50
Information Sharing and Clarification of Intent and Process 51
Dosage 57
Time requirements 58
Informed Consent Process 58
    The Areas Covered by the Informed Consent Form 59
    Confidentiality 59
Offering experiences incrementally 61
Guiding the Session 62
Number of Guides 62
Items Which Should Be Available 62
Music 64
As the Participant Arrives for the Session 65

Mark Haden

- Beginning of the Psychedelic Session 66
- Psychedelic Group Experiences 71
- Dealing with Specific Behaviours 73
    - Talking During the Beginning and Middle of the Session 73
    - Moving Around the Room 73
    - Moving Unpredictably 73
    - Asking the Guide Personal Questions 74
    - Becoming Increasingly Anxious and Agitated...............74
    - If the Participant is Extremely Emotional 75
    - Trying to Leave the Space 76
    - Going to the Bathroom 76
    - Vomiting 77
    - Urine or Bowel Release 77
    - Fire Alarm or Earthquake 77
    - Cuddling 78
    - Sexual behaviour 78
    - Spiritual Bypass 79
- During the Last Part of the Session 80
- Bringing Resolution to Turbulence 82
- at the Ending of a Session 82
- Concluding the Session 84
- Post-Session Debrief 85
- Behaviours to Avoid 85
- Offer What You Have 86
- Integration 87
    - The Goals of the Integration Process are: 87
    - The Initial Process of Integration: 88
    - Integration Over Time 90
- Code of Ethics 91
    - Integrity 91
    - Competence 91
    - Health and Safety 91
    - Healthy Boundaries 92
    - Being a Psychedelic Guide 93

Manual for Psychedelic Guides

    Ongoing Training 94
    Being a Functional Member of a Team 95
    Future psychedelic research/self-guiding. 96
    Conclusion 97
Appendix A 98
    Canyon River Canoe Analogy 98
Appendix B 102
    Relaxing Meditation 102
Appendix C 103
Appendix D 104
Source Acknowledgment 113
Suggested Reading 113
References - main text 117
Appendix D – Drug Interactions References: 121

Manual for Psychedelic Guides

Forward

Psychedelics are not for everyone, and not everyone who wants to serve psychedelics to others is necessarily qualified or skilled enough to do so without causing harm. The ecology of the modern psychedelic movement is diverse: there are therapeutic approaches, shamanic approaches, religious and spiritual approaches, psychoanalytic approaches, and recreational and personal approaches. Some individuals undergo years of training, either with a traditional shaman or provider, or perhaps as part of a therapy training program at a graduate institute. Still others, inspired by their own positive and intriguing experiences with psychedelics, develop an evangelical stance, desiring to share the magic with as many people as possible, with perhaps no training whatsoever.

The reality is that interest in, and access to, psychedelics, in both "legitimate" clinics and retreat centers, and among "underground" practitioners and providers, is growing exponentially around the planet. The Psychedelic Renaissance is well underway, and it is transforming how we look at health, spirituality, religion, wellbeing, personal growth and development, and even how we think of the nature of consciousness and the nature of reality itself. In many areas of the world, there is already legal access to psychedelic medicines in a variety of environments and experiential methodologies. In other areas of the world, legal access to psychedelic medicines is fast approaching and will soon be a prominent feature of healthcare systems and, increasingly, in spiritual and religious communities.

Traditional cultures that have utilized psychedelics for healing, spirituality, religion, and personal transformation, have thousands of years of experience and tradition to draw upon in their use of these extraordinarily powerful tools of consciousness. However, in much of the non-traditional "modern" world, use of psychedelics and

Mark Haden

practices and concerns around serving and facilitating them in experiential modalities is something of a "Wild West," where there is little conformity, oversight, or professional associations with clear guidelines and systems of ethics and best practices. While this is due, to some extent, to the often illegality of psychedelics in many countries that have been saturated in misleading and unscientific propaganda around the supposed dangers of psychedelics, it is also due to the fact that many people simply feel "called" to share the medicine and have no training, supervision or mentorship. As legal access to psychedelic medicines grow, we can expect that diverse methodologies and practices will still be present, but there will also be greater awareness around what, exactly, are not only safe and effective treatment modalities, but also what makes someone a skilled guide: what personal traits, psychological types, interpersonal behaviors, and interpretive modes are best suited to the profession.

It is to that end that Mark Haden, Executive Director of MAPS Canada (the Multidisciplinary Association of Psychedelic Studies), has produced this timely and highly relevant *Manual for Psychedelic Guides*. This book of well-sourced advice and guidelines is a *must read* for anyone who either wants to serve psychedelics, or those who already do so. Consensus is building in the psychedelic movement around best practices and harm reduction. As with any other expression of human behavior and culture, there have been abusive behaviors in psychedelic circles. Unqualified individuals have offered powerful psychedelics to those who have not been properly screened or prepared. Power-hungry individuals, and on occasion, those with abusive psychological tendencies, have been drawn to the work. This is not a reflection of psychedelics in-and-of-themselves: it is a reflection of the dynamics of human interaction and relation. The reality is that many get into the business of providing psychedelics to others with no training or little awareness of professional ethics and behavior protocols such as with

Manual for Psychedelic Guides

preparation, navigation, and the all-important, integration. In any endeavor in which there is an inherent power imbalance, which is certainly the case between psychedelic guides and participants, there is a need for guidance, supervision and at least minimal community oversight.

Anything as powerful and effective as psychedelics – and here, there is no doubt, whatsoever – needs proper guidelines, suggestions, and effective modalities, in order to maximize their healing and transformative potential, and lessen the potential dangers and pitfalls that come with the use of any kind of powerful tool.

This *Manual for Psychedelic Guides* comes at the perfect time. Here in Oregon, where I'm writing this, the initiative to legalize psilocybin ("magic mushrooms") assisted therapy just qualified for the ballot, to be voted on this coming November. Similar measures will soon be appearing across the United States, let alone across the world. Religious and spiritual use of Ayahuasca and Peyote have already been legalized within the state of Oregon. Many communities across the US are also experiencing a wave of "decriminalization" movements, where local governments are encouraged not to criminalize and prosecute use of psychedelics and "plant medicines". The sea change is already here. The time for clear guidance is not some indefinite time in the future, either near or far: it is right now. Psychedelic therapy, religion, and spirituality is here, now, and it only shows signs of increasing.

As the world moves beyond the limited and mis-informed "War on Drugs" program as initiated by the United States and reinforced by the United Nations and member states, the general public is increasingly being informed as to the efficacy and safety of psychedelic use and therapy. Anyone who has been paying attention has seen articles about psychedelics in a variety of publications, both

Mark Haden

print and online. Psychedelics are being featured with greater regularity in entertainment, movies, and television. Main characters undergo cathartic psychedelic experiences, such as was recently featured on "Billions." Celebrities like Gwyneth Paltrow feature psychedelic healing in their branded info-tainment programs. People like Mike Tyson proclaim the transformative potential of "toad medicine," 5-MeO-DMT. Even the puppeted gelflings in "The Dark Crystal" are aware that there are certain berries that only the shamans eat to enter the spirit world. The proverbial cat is out of the bag, and there will be no going back.

In order to move things forward in a positive, life-affirming, and professional way, this guide is offered to all who are interested in providing psychedelic medicines with wisdom, humility, and professional ethics and standards. May it be well-received, and spark the necessary conversations that are needed around the globe as we collectively embrace the new psychedelic reality.

Journey well!

- Martin W. Ball, Ph.D.
  Ashland, Oregon

Manual for Psychedelic Guides

Disclaimer

This manual does not intend to encourage or promote the use of any illegal substances. It is intended to be used by guides who are offering this service within the context of legal, well supervised experiences. This manual does not offer any legal, medical, psychological or professional advice. The author disclaims any liability, arising directly or indirectly, for the use of the material in this manual.

Preface – A Brief Summary of the Science

The use of psychedelics is not a new phenomenon. For millennia, cultures world-wide have respected psychedelic plants and fungi to provide healing, knowledge, creativity, celebration of transitions and spiritual connection [1-11]. Science is just beginning to catch up with what many indigenous communities have been experiencing for centuries.

Lysergic acid diethylamide (LSD) and psilocybin were two of the first psychedelic substances to show therapeutic potential in the 1960s [12]. Recent scientific studies are demonstrating how psychedelics can be beneficial for treating conditions such as end-of-life anxiety [13], substance use disorders [14-16], cluster-headaches [17], PTSD [18-20], anxiety [14], obsessive-compulsive disorder [21], treatment-resistant depression [14], chronic pain [22], and alleviating OCD (Obsessive Compulsive Disorder) [21]. Studies observing use of psychedelics in community, outside of carefully controlled lab environments, also show positive outcomes, such as reducing rates of intimate partner violence [23], recidivism [24], suicidality [25, 26], positive mood and social connectedness [27, 28] and ability to relate to nature [29]. Meta-analyses of the academic literature consistently report optimism regarding the significant potential health, social and spiritual benefits of psychedelics [16, 30-37].

The U.S. Food and Drug Administration (FDA) assessed the data and subsequently granted Breakthrough Therapy designation for two studies investigating psilocybin therapy for treatment-resistant depression and for MDMA assisted therapy for PTSD. Breakthrough designation allows the FDA to grant priority review to drug candidates if preliminary clinical trials indicate that the therapy offers substantial treatment advantages over existing options for patients with serious or life-threatening diseases.

In addition to treating a variety of conditions, psychedelics can also be valuable for personal and spiritual growth. Specifically, a Johns Hopkins study on "healthy normals" found that over 75% of the respondents considered their psilocybin experience to be one of the top five most meaningful or spiritual experiences of their lives [38, 39].

The risk of harms from psychedelics is extremely low. In 2000, a risk assessment on mushrooms containing psilocybin was conducted by the Netherlands-based Coordination Centre for the Assessment and Monitoring of new drugs and concluded that the health risk to the individuals, the public, and threats to public order was low. This has been confirmed by many researchers [40-43] and the European Monitoring Centre for Drugs and Drug Addiction [44]. David Nutt's analysis of drug harms is of specific interest, as his detailed assessment includes an exhaustive list of harms to both self and others and concludes that mushrooms, LSD and Ecstasy are three of the least harmful in a long list of both legal and illegal drugs [42].

It is notable that the Canadian Medical Association Journal choose to put an exploration of the psychedelic renaissance on the front cover of its journal which is sent to all Canadian physicians [45].

Manual for Psychedelic Guides

Psychedelics, which have been used for millennia by many indigenous cultures for healing, are now being legitimized by the tools of science in many universities. There is a wide range of different physical, psychological and social benefits being documented by modern day researchers. It is therefore predictable that the use of psychedelics will grow. Therefore, this manual is an offering to share the knowledge needed to maximize the potential benefits and minimize the potential harms of the psychedelic experience.

Choice of Language in This Manual

The term "guide" is used in reference to the individual(s) who oversee a psychedelic treatment session. The term is used broadly to describe the appropriate level of intervention in this particular therapeutic context: somewhere between the active role of a "therapist" and the inactive role of a "sitter". It is assumed that the guide is able to demonstrate the skills of both a therapist and a sitter, as appropriate. The term "guide" is also used because it encompasses individuals with a wide range of backgrounds, as psychedelic treatment sessions require a truly multidisciplinary approach.

The term "treatment" is used instead of "therapy", as it is a broader term which more accurately describes the desired "non-directive" approach.

The term "participant" is used instead of "subject", as it more accurately reflects the "active participation" and "empowerment to change", which are foundational principles in this treatment process.

"The only journey is the journey within."

- Rainer Maria Rilke

Mark Haden

Manual for Psychedelic Guides

Introduction

The practice of working with psychedelics for healing or spiritual purposes is not new. For centuries, many indigenous traditions have used "sacred medicines" in celebration of transitions (from puberty to seasonal changes), ceremonial healing and spiritual awakening. In the last few decades, guides within both research and underground communities have also been working with psychedelics in their healing practices. There are many different approaches and medicines (and combinations of medicines) which can be used in individual, group, couple and family therapy sessions. This manual is designed for individuals who are assisting others in experiencing the psychedelic effects of substances such as LSD, Psilocybin, MDMA, 3-MMC, DMT, 5-MeO-DMT, Ayahuasca and other psychedelics. It is intended to be a manual for guides using moderate to high dosages of a psychedelics in their practice. It is not intended to offer guidance to those who are involved in psycholytic therapy, which is psychotherapy enhanced with a low dose of a psychedelic.

This book is a community effort as it has been developed over many years with input from a diverse group of individuals. This manual is not intended to offer training in a specific model of therapy (e.g. Cognitive, Behavioural, Inner Child or Imago Relationship Therapy). However, it is assumed that many individuals who use this manual will be skilled practitioners in a variety of different therapeutic approaches, all of which could be enhanced by the information presented here. Having skills in the art of therapy can be helpful in navigating the complex terrain of projection, transference and countertransference, which are generally amplified by psychedelics. The development of the future profession of psychedelic psychotherapist/supervisor/guide will need a manual of best practices, to be used as a frame of reference and this book is offered as a first step in this direction.

Mark Haden

Psychedelic Guidance has three stages: preparation, experience and integration. All three stages require thoughtful attention to maximize the opportunity for a positive outcome.

Manual for Psychedelic Guides

Set and Setting

The existing scientific, clinical, and anthropological/spiritual literature exploring the use of psychedelics emphasizes the importance of "set" and "setting". The thoughtful incorporation of these parameters is integral to maximizing the therapeutic benefits, maintaining ethical boundaries, and avoiding untoward effects.

"Set" refers to the mental state or mindset of the participant: their beliefs, hopes, fears, personality, cultural background and expectations formed through their interactions with their world. It is commonly associated with the process of advanced psychological preparation of the participant. The term "set" also refers to the state of mind a participant is in on the day of psychedelic ingestion.

The "setting" of the experience refers to the external environment in which the session takes place. This parameter is also important, as it can affect the felt sense of psychological safety of the participant before and during the session. As such, the space should be professional, private, safe, attractively decorated, relaxing and comfortable.

The space needs to be equipped with a music system and headphones to play a music playlist. Participants will be encouraged to recline on a comfortable sofa or bed, with their eyes covered, for the majority of the session, though there should be thoughtful consideration given to the preferences of the clients. Using appropriate music and limiting external visual distraction with the use of eyeshades, tends to facilitate the manifestation of a deeply personal, inward experience.

Creating a supportive set and setting also requires:

1. Building a relationship between the participant and the guiding team (or individual), in order to develop rapport, safety and trust.

2. Ensuring a familiar, secure and comfortable environment, physically, psychologically, and socially.

Manual for Psychedelic Guides

Space Issues

Interview room

The interview space, where all the initial screening, preparation sessions and integration processes are conducted, should be comfortable with normal chairs and a desk, for ease of documentation. The "experience space" should be different from the interview and preparation spaces. Entering the "experience space" should signal a transition to a different way of being.

Experience room

Plants, specifically flowers (a rose is traditional), offer the presence of beauty and nature. Being inside a warm, safe and private environment allows the participant (and the guides) to be free from worries about interruption and facilitates the desired inward experience for the participant. All equipment and personnel should be easily accessible for the safe implementation of the process.

Ideally, this room would be large enough to accommodate a single bed, two comfortable chairs and a small desk. It should be soundproofed, or at least situated in a location where sound from within the room would not be a concern. Sound transmission to others who are not involved in the process should be limited (or preferably non-existent).

If renovation or a custom-built room is an option, sound proofing entails:

- All walls should be double, specifically made of two rows of disconnected (at least 1" apart) studs (at least 2x4 studs) with sound-proof-laminated drywall on three of the 4 possible surfaces,

Mark Haden

- Sound proof specific insulation (often green) – added between the all studs of both walls,

- Two (yes 2!) layers of sound-proof specific laminated drywall on the interior drywall - do a rough fill in cracks with drywall mud on both of the layers. Make sure that the joints of the first layer of drywall do not line up with the joints of the second layer of drywall, with no space left between the wall and the concrete slab above or the drywall ceiling),

- Mastic on all the joints between the 2x4s and the walls, floors and ceilings

- If there are windows – triple paned with laminated sound proof glass

- Doors can be soundproofed in a number of ways (e.g. double doors, sealing – solid material, sand-filled).

The experience room can be decorated to look like a comfortable, relaxing, living room, with inspirational or generic spiritual art (e.g. nature scenes, balancing rocks, birds flying, soft tapestries).

If the space is intended to be used for group experiences, there are a number of considerations. Participants should be able to move easily between sitting and lying positions. As back support is commonly needed, pillows against a wall or "festival seats" which offer support while sitting on the ground are useful. Blankets, pillows and foam pads need to be easily available. Soft blankets are preferable to sleeping bags, which can have weather protective covers that are noisy when moved.

Manual for Psychedelic Guides

Washroom for subjects and staff

Easy access to a private washroom is important. Ideally, the bathroom should be directly connected to the experience room. But a bathroom nearby would be acceptable, as long as it can be guaranteed that there will be no interaction with others on the way.

Lighting

As lighting needs to be variable, lamps with dimmers are ideal. Overhead lighting is problematic as the subject will be lying down and looking up, but may be acceptable if they can be softened sufficiently with the addition of dimmer switches.

Mark Haden

Ritualizing the Process

Metzner [46] has explored different elements of psychedelic rituals (e.g. singing, chanting, drumming, working with "sacred" objects) often used in a wide variety of indigenous traditions. A ritualistic approach to a psychedelic session has some advantages in focusing the participant and ensuring psychological stability. Rituals can be imbued with a wide variety of meanings and can therefore make the experience personally meaningful for the participant. As healing and spiritual rituals can be quite generic they can be modified and shaped to accommodate the unique healing or spiritual needs of each individual.

Rituals can be powerful in creating a container of safety. They can be used as appropriate in response to distress or challenging behaviour. A singing bowl or gong, for example, when used thoughtfully by the guides, can be used to signify moments of change and transition. In this context, music can also be particularly important. Communicating with music is cross-cultural and free from the complexities of possible misinterpretations and disagreements, which can easily occur in verbal communication. Furthermore, as the possibility of misunderstanding words is amplified in altered states of consciousness, music is a more appropriate means of communication as the interpretation of music is universal.

An example of appropriate communication with music is found in Ayahuasca ceremonies where traditional Amazonian shamans interact with music with Westerners who are seeking healing. If the ceremonies involved verbal communication, the different world views are more likely to come into conflict. For instance, shamans often believe that psychological problems are the result of "bad spirits", while the western belief system attributes them to issues like past trauma. Such conflicts can be particularly disruptive in

Manual for Psychedelic Guides

psychedelic states. Therefore, when music is the medium of communication, the disagreements are minimized, and the possibility of healing is enhanced.

While rituals can be powerful in bringing safety and meaning to the experience, they can also be problematic. If the rituals are not "in sync" with the participant, the value of the rituals can actually be negative. This can happen if some aspects of the rituals are in direct conflict with the beliefs of the participant and ritual feels as if it as an imposition. Problems arise with the assumption that beliefs and values are shared. For example, the guide may want to do something as seemingly benign as "calling in the ancestors and spirit guides" to help facilitate a session, but the participant may be a staunch atheist. In this case it would be important to recognize that not everyone who seeks psychedelic treatment is in agreement with metaphysical or spiritual beliefs. For some, too much ritual can be alienating and off-putting. In order for rituals to be truly meaningful, there needs to be some degree of agreement on the meanings behind symbols, practices and beliefs.

Furthermore, the attitude of the guide towards the ritual is also an important aspect to consider. If, for example, the guide believes that their particular brand of ritual is special, the healing is then attributed to the healer and not the participant. This can be a disempowering experience for the participant and can hinder the therapeutic effects of the psychedelic session itself. Rituals that are inflexible and maladaptive to changing circumstances can also have negative impacts. For example, an Ayahuascaro who refuses to use disposable cups, as they don't fit the standard ritual when working with participants with a history of addiction and high rates of Hep C and HIV infections, can increase disease transmission. In such a case, the explanation that "this is our tradition" is poor consolation for anyone who becomes newly infected due to such inflexibility.

Mark Haden

Therefore, skillful use of rituals requires guides to be adaptable. Guides should also remind themselves of the importance of humility and the understanding that the healing comes from the participants themselves, not the guide. To maximize the healing potential of the experience, ritual practices and the meanings behind them should be discussed before committing to the session. Based on this discussion, rituals can be added, deleted or adapted to suit specific participants. Guides should be flexible in the type and amount of ritualistic structures they bring to the session.

Manual for Psychedelic Guides

Presence and Intentions

Set and setting are influenced by the totality of the body, mind, and spirit of the guide and this includes assumptions, intentions, knowledge, presence, actions, skill sets, personalities and intuitions. Individuals come to this work from a variety of training backgrounds, professional disciplines, and philosophical orientations, and this is important, as a wide variety of skills, interests, and experiences are beneficial to the development of best practices and optimal skill development for the field as a whole.

Effective psychedelic guides facilitate the journey into the unconsciousness where both humanity's deepest fears and boundless love reside. By bringing our full presence and integrity toward the participant, guided by science and informed by the knowledge and skill of those with more experience, psychedelic guides have the ability to facilitate powerful transformations. Instead of acting as over-active interventionists, guides serve more as caring witnesses to provide safety and comfort without intrusion. Guides first establish rapport and trust with the participant, and then ensure a container of safety is created and maintained for all. Guides are also responsible for offering a safe, aesthetically pleasing, comfortable setting.

When non-ordinary states of consciousness are experienced, guides must remain steady and centered as this is the vital counterbalance to the participant's turbulent experiences. It is essential that the guides engender warm solidity and infuse the setting with a sense of stability and safety. They must also be knowledgeable about the specific medicine they are using.

Skillful guides appreciate that they are on the journey together with the participant, who they acknowledge as a brave individual who journeys into the unknown, and sometimes find themselves in psychological terrain which is difficult and scary to navigate. The shared experiences which are reflected on in retrospect may be useful not only for the participant's growth and awareness, but also for the evolving skill of the guide.

Manual for Psychedelic Guides

Inner Healing Intelligence

Inner Healing Intelligence is a concept used throughout this manual. This concept was originally developed by Stanislof Grof and refined by Michael and Annie Mithoefer, who have made it central to the MAPS (Multidisciplinary Association for Psychedelic Studies) MDMA-assisted treatment process. This concept is used to help the participant connect with their innate ability to heal and grow, and to empower them to be responsible for their own healing. Turbulent and often difficult emotional processes may be easier to work with and resolve when understood to be part of the Inner Healing Intelligence. The following explanation may be helpful in discussing the concept with participants:

> The body initiates a remarkably complex and sophisticated healing process, and always spontaneously attempts to move toward healing, as evidenced by the inevitable healing of a cut or a bruise, for example. The psyche too exhibits an innate healing intelligence and capacity, which is revealed by psychedelic medicine.

Guides who understand the concept of the Inner Healing Intelligence are less active (and more empowering) than therapists who believe that it is their interactions with the participant that result in the healing process.

"Your self-worth is determined by you. You don't have to depend on someone telling you who you are."

- Beyonce

Mark Haden

The Role of the Guide

The role of the guide is to attend to the needs (physical, personal, interpersonal) of participants while creating an atmosphere of stability, compassion and safety while avoiding "care-taking", fixing, labeling, psychoanalysis, diagnosing, or being distracted.

Qualities of Guides

A Knowledgeable, Skilled and Wise Guide:

- Has the experience, knowledge and wisdom to understand the degree of activity required. What is needed is a balance between an "inactive sitter" and an "overactive guide", and understanding that either of these roles can be required during the session.

- Knows when and how to assist the process, and when not to intervene.

- Has the ability to stay relaxed, calm and grounded in the presence of fear, intense anxiety, turbulent emotions, or other mental states that may be expressed emotionally or physically.

- Has an understanding of the pharmacology (e.g., mechanism of action, typical timing of onset, duration), and range of different effects of the medicine.

- Trusts both the psychedelic medicine and the participant's internal healer.

- Has full appreciation of being alive, lives a life with both meaning and purpose, understands that we are all "wounded healers" and can reflect on some of the agonies and ecstasies of human existence.

Manual for Psychedelic Guides

Experiential Knowledge:

- Understands that encounters in the realms of the unconscious can be transcendent, meaningful, significant and life-transforming.

- Is able to avoid using labels such as "psychosis", "freaking out", or "bad trip", and can respond with understanding and compassion to a wide range of behaviours and perceptions.

- Understands from their own experiences, the benefits that can be obtained from altered states of consciousness.

- Has an ability to shift between modes of being, from a scientist, to a poet, to simply a warm compassionate presence.

- Appreciates that all psychedelic experiences are like works of art, created in collaboration with the participant and that each session is unique and evolves in unpredictable ways which can, in retrospect, be seen as perfect in the exploration of important life insights and lessons.

Knowledge of the Human Mind When Seen Through the Lens of Psychedelics

Guides should be aware of the range of different theories that have been developed to understand the nature of the conscious and unconscious mind as it manifests under the illumination of psychedelics. These models are still under development and can be wide-ranging. For example, followers of Grof observe the Basic Perinatal Matrices, while Freudians observe Oedipal complexes, Jungians see through the lens of archetypes, and neuroscientists see the suppression of the Default Mode Network. Similarly, understanding indigenous models is also helpful. Many shamans for example, understand that the abyss of consciousness is filled with entities, spirits, and beings, who interact with the participant in psychedelic states. Some spirits are neutral, some beneficial, and some are harmful. Ideas of possession, channelling, messages, and communication are supported by this perspective. Additionally, understanding the nondual mode of consciousness is valuable. From this perspective it is observed that consciousness is unitary and is a reflective mirror of interactions between different levels of the unitary self where nothing is seen as "other". Christopher Bache's work, exploring his multi-decade high dose LSD experiences, is an important read for anyone who wants to understand both how sequential psychedelic experiences can progress and how these medicines can help us to understand our lives in a larger spiritual context [47].

An understanding of a wide variety of different theories is helpful for any guide who supports the psychedelic experience.

Knowledge of the Power and Importance of Human Relationships

- Guides should follow all relevant professional codes of ethics, in addition to the specific ethical guidelines outlined below.

- Guides should maintain non-manipulative, non-exploitative relationships and keep appropriate personal and professional boundaries.

- Guides should understand transference (perceiving the projections from a participant) and countertransference (owning one's own projections about a participant) and should be able to demonstrate the ability to self-reflect on, and discuss, these issues as needed.

- Guides should understand the power imbalance that inevitably occurs in the relationship between the participant (who is extremely disclosing and vulnerable) and the guide (who is seen as being the "wise one"). There are a number of possible concerns here, as an immature guide can easily start to believe

Manual for Psychedelic Guides

that they have the answers and see themselves as "THE great therapist". This attitude is likely to be detrimental to the psychedelic healing process. The appropriate response is humility (not ego inflation) and an openness to learn from the participant, with the ability to see the participant's issues as being a normal part of our shared humanity. Metzner (2015) cautions guides to be ever aware of the potential of their own grandiosity and of over-idealizing their own perceptions of what is meaningful, in the states of consciousness associated with psychedelic-assisted treatment. As prevention is better than damage control, an open and ongoing discussion among guides on this issue (e.g. during staff meetings) is advisable to build and maintain healthy team dynamics.

Appreciation of Human Suffering

- Guides should have an appreciation of the "Dark Night of the Soul" as a healing part of the spiritual journey of a life fully lived. The concept of a "wounded healer" is helpful as we all have our own degrees of suffering and this understanding helps the guide to maintain humility.

- Guides should provide a steady level of warmth and compassion during any pain experienced by the participant (physical and psychological).

- Guides should have an appreciation of the limitations of language. Participants often describe the experience as having an ineffable and paradoxical quality, beyond words and encompassing truths that otherwise seem incompatible or contradictory. For example, one may have an altered perception of time and be unable to describe the experience.

- Similarly, a participant may have difficulty making coherent and intelligible speech while the psychedelic medicine is in effect.

> **God grant me the serenity to accept the things I cannot change, courage to change the things I can, and wisdom to know the difference**
> - *AA Serenity Prayer*

Manual for Psychedelic Guides

The Skills of Being a Psychedelic Guide

The guide serves as a steady and supportive presence for the participants. Authenticity and self-awareness are an integral part of creating a warm and safe set and setting. The guide's distinctive personal signature contributes to this role through specific gifts, skills, training, attitude, and experience. A guide's full presence is instrumental during preparatory meetings, on the day the participant ingests the medicine and during the integration follow-up meetings.

In James Miller's book, *The Art of Being a Healing Presence,* we are reminded that the guide's presence, stability, warmth and compassion is more important to the outcome than the techniques employed. Training to be a guide means practicing being fully present on this path of learning and provides us with precious insights into ourselves, our motivations and all of our relationships.

> "We connect through listening. A loving silence often has far more power than words."

A guide should be in control of their own ego, identity, personality traits, and default reactivity. They should hold an unwavering faith in both themselves and the participant. They provide reassurance, and ensure that safety is maintained, but understand that "care-taking" or "fixing" is not needed. They do not take personal responsibility for the experience, or the outcome, other than their own behaviour. They are able to attend to the participant's feelings, without getting caught up in, or overwhelmed by their own.

The guide should have already explored, accepted, and become open to the experience of mystical and spiritual terrain. The concept of "oceanic boundlessness" should be familiar. Skillful guides provide a starting point, and then gently encourage the participant to "relax, breathe, stay with your experience", instead of resisting. As a result, the participant is emboldened to dive deeply into their unconscious mind and transpersonal experiences, to accept whatever shows up, and be curious about where their mind is taking them. It is important to trust that they are receiving what they need most at that time. Guiding is most akin to simply "*Being With*". This is a quiet, precious, and very powerful gift. While a common description of this process is "holding space" a more accurate statement is "being present".

The ability to be fully present for someone may be simple but it is far from easy. We are used to doing many things at once, overfilling our days with activities, emails and cell phones. Our minds have nonstop chatter and to-do lists, and staying in the moment – being present NOW – is an essential skill to have in this work. Presence can be hard to identify because it usually doesn't entail a lot of activity. By being present in a psychedelic context, we simply accompany the participant as they "get in and through" their experience. Being present gives permission to usher in whatever wants to happen on its own accord, trusting in the participant's innate ability to move toward whatever they need. Knowledgeable guides are aware that each psychedelic experience is unique and unpredictable.

Being present sounds simple, but is not easy as we live in a world of "text beeps", internet distractions and fear-based news feeds. To be present requires time, energy, and balanced, focused awareness. The path to learning this process is not complicated. Start by keeping your eyes open, experience your ordinary senses and your body sensations. Notice the complex sensations of breathing, in the throat, chest and stomach. Notice where you are, right now, taking in all that is around you at this moment. At times, you may close your eyes to deepen a meditative state of awareness. Pay complete, mindful attention to each separate sense, one at a time. What sounds, sights and feelings are present within you and in the environment? Refine your observational skills by paying attention to the details. It takes persistence, discipline, and effort to quiet one's mind-chatter. Being in the "here and now" requires discipline and repetition, and most of us need continual reminders, and lots of practice. The more we work at being completely present, the more natural it becomes. The more we wake up to what is around us and within us, the more we are apt

Manual for Psychedelic Guides

to remain centered and supportive. This is why it is important to include experiential portions in all guide training, and why guides are encouraged to have a personal meditation practice, and familiarity with altered states of consciousness.

Being present is a skill that can be developed, practiced, and continuously cultivated. It is like a fragile plant which needs frequent care and attention to flourish and will wither and die if ignored.

The guide is a midwife for the spirit.

It is important to develop insights into our own transference and countertransference, or filters through which we see the world. While these filters can be both positive and negative, they cannot be avoided as we all have our own histories and unconscious reactions to people and the world around us. Open, self-disclosing and honest supervision and debriefing these issues is especially important. The more you know about yourself the more likely you are to be able to stay centered and tranquil throughout the session. When you are understanding, accepting and comfortable with yourself it will be easier for the participant to transition from one state of consciousness to another. After reviewing hundreds of sessions in different settings, Timothy Leary and Richard Alpert (Ram Dass) concluded that, in most situations, participants became distressed when the guide had become unsettled, uncertain or upset.

Check in with yourself. Ask yourself what emotions you are feeling. Lack of centered presence manifests as fidgeting, closed or tense body postures, indulging in distractions, mental absence, excessive internal dialog, the need to engage in normal social activities, respond to a text or catch up with work, etc. Be aware, as participants experience different energies, thoughts, emotions, and somatic experiences, that you, as a guide, are likely to feel your own reactions to these changes in your body, emotions and thought patterns. Being a guide can mean that you, to some degree, will need to move through these experiences as well, in your own way. Your job is to allow yourself to feel these changes without reacting or letting yourself be drawn into them, pulling you out of being present for the participant.

The only thing we can know is that we know nothing and that is the highest flight of human wisdom.

- Leo Tolstoy

Manual for Psychedelic Guides

The Six Core Competencies

In her exploration of the skills required for psychedelic guides, Phelps [48] outlines 6 competencies:

1) Empathetic Abiding Presence

Contemporary models focus on the empathy of the guide: an empathetic responsivity that has been leavened into the embodiment of a calm, abiding presence during psychedelic treatment. This capacity is evidenced in the guide during preparation, the session itself, and integration meetings. The term "abiding" here is purposely used to convey the idea of a witness to the mystery of life in action, during psychedelic-assisted psychotherapy. Components of the empathetic abiding presence are diverse and include:

- Composure
- Evenly suspended attention
- Mindfulness
- Empathetic listening
- "Doing by non-doing"
- Responding to distress with calmness
- Equanimity

The goal is to offer oneself as a witness from a loving presence.

Empathetic listeners are relaxed, but engaged, ask questions, and explore without prying. The listener maintains appropriate eye contact and offers appropriate, reassuring touches, if culturally and personally acceptable. Empathetic listeners may be required to admit that they don't have answers. Important components of empathetic listening and active listening are:

- Minimal encouragement, verbal and non-verbal

- Invitation rather than direction

- Paraphrasing

- Reflecting

- Emotional labeling

- Validating

- Reassurance and waiting

- Allowing participants to come to conclusions themselves

One of the attributes which helps guides to develop an empathetic presence is a strongly developed interoception (body sensation awareness). Self-awareness (of both body, emotions and mind) helps to put one's own personal issues aside and focus on the needs of another.

2) **Trust Enhancement**

A guide should be skilled in enhancing trust in three arenas: the participant's view of the guide as trustworthy; the participant's trust in their own inner healing capacity; to reliably normalize for the participant the fact that radically unexpected moments can occur in sessions, and are trusted as part of the process. Such capacity of trust-enhancement enables the guide to support the participants' engagement, in making meaningful sense of their lives and inner healing processes.

Manual for Psychedelic Guides

3) Spiritual Intelligence

Guides who are competent in psychedelic-assisted treatment have knowledge and values that can be described as a "spiritual intelligence" that go beyond conventional psychological development. In addition to self-awareness, it implies having an awareness of our relationship to the transcendent, to each other, to the earth, and to all beings. The ability to calm one's own internal dialogue and relax the body with meditative techniques is important, as many hours go by simply watching the participant lying motionless. If the guide is distracted, the participant, who becomes very sensitive to interpersonal dynamics, will not feel their supportive presence. Spiritual intelligence is always a "work in progress" and spending quiet guiding time wisely helps to develop this attribute.

4) Knowledge

Psychedelic guides should be competent in their knowledge of anatomy, physiology, neurobiology, pharmacology, drug disposition and interactions, and neuropharmacology of psychedelic drugs. Familiarity with clinical narratives on the normative effects of different psychedelic drugs at varying dosage, in a variety of sets and settings, is highly instructive as well.

5) Self-Awareness and Ethical Integrity

This competency relates to six components of the guide's acumen related to:

- Self-awareness of personal motives for this work
- Integrity in protecting boundaries with the participants
- Well-developed capacities for building therapeutic alliances
- Skills in attachment theories
- Skills in transference-countertransference analysis
- Personal self-care

A core component of this competency is a capacity to wisely reflect on one's motives when conducting psychedelic therapy, while simultaneously working with participants' attachment and transference processes. Understanding one's own strengths and areas of growth is also needed.

6) Proficiency in complementary techniques

The primary component of this competency are the acquisition of skills and knowledge that form a toolbox of complementary therapeutic methods, to be used in various phases of the entire process. Many types of complementary therapeutic skills are useful across all stages of psychedelic therapy. They can be used to understand participant readiness in the early preparation phase, to bring closure for the participant within the psychedelic session itself, or for debriefing and analysis during integration sessions. These

Manual for Psychedelic Guides

additional skills and therapeutic methods can include somatic-oriented techniques, Holotropic Breathwork, stress inoculation, therapeutic body work, techniques of eye-gazing at a mirror or with the guide, felt sensing and focusing, somatic experiencing and sensorimotor therapies. The complementary techniques will be different for different guides, but all guides on the team should have a basic understanding and ability to support the complementary techniques used by other members.

Mark Haden

Trauma Resolution skills

Many presenting issues, like depression, anxiety and anger, often have trauma as their underlying cause. Therefore, it is important to be equipped with an understanding of trauma, along with skills which help in trauma resolution.

This is critical for individuals who work with clients entering into altered states of consciousness since there is an increased likelihood that repressed trauma may rise to the surface of consciousness. This presents *either* 1) a tremendous opportunity for healing, or, 2) the possibility that traumatic imprints merely recycle and potentially reinforce and further entrench themselves in the client's nervous system.

While a full explanation of trauma-informed therapeutic skillsets is beyond the scope of this guide book, the reader is encouraged to review the work of Peter Levine, Pat Ogden, Diane Poole Heller, Sharon Stanley and Mariah Moser.

What is Trauma?

Trauma occurs when a person is overwhelmed by events *or* enduring circumstances, experiences fear or helplessness, and their natural drive to cope is overridden. Put simply, from the perspective of the nervous system, trauma is "too much, too fast, too soon". This causes the nervous system to enter into survival mode, into 'hyperarousal' and/or 'collapse/play dead' states (also known as fight, flight or freeze).

Understanding the Origins of Trauma

The medical diagnosis of "Post Traumatic Stress Disorder" (PTSD), is only a very specific and severe set of symptoms that represents the

Manual for Psychedelic Guides

tip of the iceberg of the broader spectrum of trauma symptoms people experience.

Trauma does not just stem from going to war or being a victim of an assault or life-threatening accident. Trauma also frequently happens in early childhood, and we lack understanding about its near ubiquity and impact. In his book "The Trauma of Everyday Life" psychiatrist Dr. Mark Epstein explains how trauma does not just happen to a few unlucky people, but is a very common experience.

Children, particularly in infancy and early childhood, are exquisitely sensitive and 100% dependent upon their adult caregivers for survival. Thus, attaching to their adult caregivers is a survival imperative, and they will do so with whomever is present, at any cost. Children are therefore particularly vulnerable to trauma, especially attachment trauma (e.g. death of parent, adoption, etc.) and developmental trauma (psycho-emotional neglect, or other kinds of abuses that occur over extended periods, and thus significantly affect the developing brain). According to traumatologist, Dr. Alan Schore, childhood emotional neglect is the most serious form of trauma, since it represents a denial of our fundamental humanity. A vulnerable child feels alone, separated, isolated, and alienated (contrary to our nature as mammals) and is effectively denied the relational environment necessary for healthy brain development.

Trauma is the "Ever Present Past" existing NOW, in the body

Peter Levine is known for pointing out that trauma is not about what happened in the past, but how that event is held, or 'frozen in time', unresolved in the nervous system, in the present moment. He points us to the importance of working with the ways past traumas show up in the body, moment by moment, in real time, which creates opportunities for those imprints to be 'renegotiated,' so they can be released and transformed. *Renegotiation* is a term coined by Peter Levine to describe a process whereby new pathways are created for bound trauma energy to complete its movement and course of action.

Trauma can be Spiritual

Gabor Maté (a Vancouver physician and author) defines trauma as "a fundamental disconnect from Self/Source," meaning from one's truest and deepest nature. He explains that the problem with trauma is not what happened, but how what happened caused a person to disconnect from their Essence. Trauma healing can thus be a very deep and rich path for a person to remember or rediscover who and what they actually are, which is how many people define the spiritual path.

Physical Touch

Most therapists have been trained to believe that touching a client/participant is inappropriate and can be crossing a boundary. Nonetheless, when working with psychedelics, non-sexual touch can be very helpful in the healing process. In fact, it can be problematic if touch is not offered when requested, as this means not responding appropriately to the therapeutic needs of the participant. Body work, hand-holding, and hugging can be an important part of the therapeutic process when it is welcomed or clearly invited by the participant. It is important to discuss the distinction between sexual and non-sexual healing touch in the preparation sessions. If touch is offered, it is important to do it slowly, by offering a hand at first (for example), and waiting to see if the invitation to touch is accepted. Initiating rapid touch without being sure that it is welcomed can be perceived as intrusive.

Manual for Psychedelic Guides

Eye Contact

Understanding the experience that accompanies various types of eye contact is important. Looking someone directly in the eye, for example, can invite reflection on the connection between the participant and the guide, which can distract from the process of inner exploration. Alternatively, a "soft gaze" where the guide looks slightly down can be less distracting to the participant and allow them to maintain inward focus.

Under specific circumstances, however, the opposite can also be helpful. Specifically, "eye gazing", or prolonged direct eye contact, can offer a participant strong concentration, allowing for unconscious psychic material to be projected onto the guide. Intense, focused eye gazing can create an opportunity for the participant to go deeper into understanding an external relationship (e.g. with a parent, partner or child). The offer to "eye gaze" should be tentative. If accepted the guide should be sensitive to the participant's need to end the process. The different types of eye contact should be discussed and practiced during the preparatory phase.

Body Language

An open body language can convey connection and support, without distracting the participant from their internal reflective process. Body language can change depending on what is happening for the participant. This is only relevant if the participant has removed their eyeshades.

Mark Haden

Therapeutic Alliance

In order to create and maintain a safe, collaborative, therapeutic alliance with the participant, it is crucial that guides maintain self-awareness. Guides must be empathetically present during the participant's experience, yet at the same time maintain healthy, appropriate boundaries. In doing so, guides encourage the participant to stay present with her/his own inner experience, and create a safe environment for them to explore new and unexpected perceptions that may arise during the healing process. The strength of the therapeutic experience greatly depends on the guides' level of comfort with intense emotions, and their skill in remaining present, empathetic, and open to a range of emotional experiences.

As empathic listeners, guides attend to the participant's account of her/his inner experience, the meaning behind them, and any ambivalent thoughts and feelings. Guides keep in mind any intentions that the participant identified during introductory and preparatory meetings, while also allowing for additional, perhaps unexpected psychic material to emerge. They also consider individual psychological factors (such as attachment styles, transference and countertransference issues) that may impact the therapeutic relationship and inform the specific type and amount of therapeutic intervention that will be best suited for that individual.

Manual for Psychedelic Guides

In order to maintain the delicate balance between inner focus and providing a safe space for exploration in an open-ended way, guides must respect the Inner Healing Intelligence of the participant's own psyche and body, skillfully interweaving periods of interaction with periods of silent witnessing.

Participants naturally want to get the maximum benefit from their sessions. As such, they may often need to be reminded of the paradox that healing is best accomplished by surrendering to the process, rather than trying to direct it. They should also be reminded that important insights and healing often arise through a non-linear process that may shift perceptions and resolve conflicts in unexpected ways. This process is enhanced by the participant's trust that their Inner Healing Intelligence in conjunction with the medicine, will bring forth whatever experiences are needed for healing and growth. As such anything that arises is seen as part of the healing process. In this vein, the participant is encouraged to surrender to the process as fully as possible, and not to "get ahead of the medicine" with efforts to direct it. Paradoxically, the guide's role is often to follow, rather than guide the participant. At times, it may be helpful for guides to remind the participant that facing painful experiences is a path toward healing.

The guide may provide verbal reassurance when needed, and nurturing touch if requested, as the participant faces potentially overwhelming thoughts, memories, or feelings. However, care should be taken not to interrupt the participant's process unnecessarily, or to convey any lack of trust in the participant's own inner healing ability. Guides should track their own emotional reactions and refrain from intervening in response to their own needs.

Men can starve from a lack of self-realization as much as they can from a lack of bread.

- Richard Wright

Should a Guide Take a Psychedelic at the Same Time as the Participant?

There are different opinions on whether the guide should take a psychedelic at the same time as the participant. While there is no right answer, it is important to consider the advantages and disadvantages. It is common (but not universal) in indigenous traditions for the guide to take psychedelic medicine with the participant. Generally, guides take a much lower dose so they "have a foot in both worlds" and can therefore function in "normal" space. Some guides observe that joining the client in the space in this way enhances connection and rapport.

The standard practice in the research community is for guides to refrain from partaking in the psychedelic experience with the participant. Researchers observe that as the guide often has to go back to their family at the end of the day, taking psychedelics could impair their functioning at home. Furthermore, if they are guiding frequently, taking a substance almost daily may have health or psychological consequences. Clinical research standards, which are informed by scientific practices, follow the standard that the physician/therapist/guide does not take the medicine they are offering to the patient.

Should the Guide Have Personal Experiences with Psychedelics

Both the research community and indigenous communities agree that a guide who has never experienced a psychedelic will lack the ability to understand, empathize, or have rapport with participants. However, guides should be mindful not to project their own experiences or expectations of psychedelics onto the participant.

Manual for Psychedelic Guides

Who Should Not Be a Psychedelic Guide?

As with all professions, some individuals are not well matched to the field of psychedelic guiding. There are (at least) four potential problems which can impact those involved with this work, and understanding these could be useful in screening out potentially harmful psychedelic guides. An open discussion about these issues is also helpful, as it assists those who may be receiving this service to be more discerning and avoid problematic situations. Discussing these challenging and hard-to-talk-about issues is important as it can reduce the incidence of these concerns.

Great Therapist Syndrome

Some individuals offering psychedelic guiding have a problematic self-perception which could be described as "THE Great Therapist Syndrome". The cause of this problem is rooted in the interaction between the therapist and the participant. Those seeking help from a therapist or guide often need to believe that the therapist (or guide) lives comfortably in the realms between human and angel. If you are going to reveal your inner most secrets, and bare your soul, a belief that the guide is really, really special, is important in the creation of feelings of safety. Most therapists understand this is a normal process and do not take it personally. On the other hand, however, some therapists, based on their own personal history, are sometimes led to believe that this projection from the participant is "real" and that they really are a "Great Therapist". This process is problematic for two reasons. First, in the hope of fostering healthy work environments, having a "Great Therapist" in a staff meeting reduces the likelihood of inclusive, positive, collegial staff relationships as Great Therapists are not skilled at listening to colleagues. Another reason the Great Therapist Syndrome is problematic is that they really believe that they are the source of the healing and consequently they send the wrong message to the participant. It is hard to witness the participant's inner healer if the guide really believes that they are the source of the healing. A truly skilled therapist is humble as they sit in witness of the participant's own inner healing process. In stark contrast, a Great Therapist can be disempowering of those seeking healing as they attribute the healing process to themselves, not the participant. As psychedelics amplify unconscious material and projections, the problem of the Great Therapist is significantly increased when psychedelic medicines are involved.

Predator

Some therapists (or guides) are attracted to work that involves vulnerable or disempowered individuals because the feelings of "having power over" can be appealing. Working with psychedelics is very attractive to these particular guides because of the high level of vulnerability of those under the influence of a psychedelic. This attraction to vulnerable people is a common feature of those with predatory inclinations and their behaviour results in a wide variety of boundary incursions from sexual abuse to emotional transgressions. In these situations, predators do not have the ability to meet the needs of the participant, as their own empowerment needs are prioritized. Furthermore, psychedelics amplify the predator problem due to the increased level of openness and emotional vulnerability of the participant during the psychedelic experience. The greater the vulnerability, the more predators are attracted.

Over-Bonding Problem

Some psychedelics are empathogens or strong bonding agents. When used skillfully, this chemical connection can be wonderful. A strong alliance between the guide and the participant is a good predictor of positive outcomes. Unfortunately, this bond can also be

Manual for Psychedelic Guides

problematic and has a significant potential downside. Guides (or therapists) who are not skillful at being explicit about their boundaries can become emotionally enmeshed which can lead to problematic emotional, physical or sexual behaviour. Guides who have current challenges with their own intimate relationships are specifically susceptible. When called to account, often therapists state "I fell in love", but this statement never justifies the boundary transgressions.

Trauma Projection

Some guides are attracted to this work as they have a significant personal trauma history and their own personal therapeutic experiences attracts them to this field. If they have not completed their own healing journey they will tend to see the world as being full of abusers and victims. This process of seeing trauma everywhere causes two problems. First, collegial dynamics can be challenging as healthy colleagues are seen as abusers and/or victims, and this is counter-productive to the creation of positive work relationships. The second problem is that the trauma filter prevents an accurate understanding of the participant's psychological issues. For example, if the guide is fixed on seeing the participant as a victim, it is hard to see the participant's potential abusive behaviour.

Psychedelics are powerful tools which can both amplify healing, when used skillfully, or promote harm when in the hands of those without the required knowledge, skills, and wisdom. This leads to the obvious conclusion that some individuals should not work with psychedelic medicines. Those who really believe they are The Great Therapist (which disempowers participants and makes them difficult colleagues due to their self-aggrandisement), those who are attracted to the vulnerable on whom they can prey, those who do not have clear boundaries, and those who have not healed from their own trauma history, should seriously consider other lines of work.

Mark Haden

Knowing yourself is the beginning of all wisdom.

- Aristotle

Manual for Psychedelic Guides

Initial Sessions

The goal of the initial process is to screen the participant, share information, clarify intent, establish an agreement on the process, document informed consent, and build a connection (of trust and safety) between the guide and the participant. The guide should meet with the participant as often as needed during the preparation process, to ensure that all the above goals are achieved. It is common practise to have two to four meetings (one to two hours each) for this process.

The guide should facilitate a clear mindset for the participant by familiarizing them with the setting, developing a trusting relationship, and exploring with them who they are, where they come from, where they currently are in life, how they cope, and what they hope to get from their participation. The guide should become familiar with the participant's intentions, goals, curiosities, their questions, any fears or worries about their body, their safety, potential behaviours, and their inner psyche. Although the unexpected may arise on the day of the session, pre-emptively uncovering what lies beneath the surface paves the way for a more comfortable and potentially deeper experience, particularly with any escalating doses. A well-structured session, with a guide that is fully present in a supportive context, makes it far more likely that a psychedelic experience will be meaningful, healthy and life-enhancing.

Psychedelic experiences are not for everyone and to avoid doing harm (to either the participant or the guide) skillful screening, based on good information, is important. Below are some red flags and green flags to look out for when screening participants.

Red Flags

Researchers have lists of issues (exclusion criteria) which are used to exclude potential subjects that are inappropriate for psychedelic research. Guides who use psychedelics have a list of issues that flag potential for unfavorable treatment outcomes. Here we discuss "red flags". It is wise to be especially careful with participants who check one or several of the following boxes. These issues warrant further investigation. Few of them are deal breakers in terms of offering the experience, but they may indicate a poor match of participant and guide, or a less than optimal outcome. Red flags should alert you to the fact that there may be concerns and it might be a good idea to slow things down, schedule some more preliminary sessions, and do more investigation.

1) Underage - the participant should be legally and emotionally an adult.

2) Unstable life (including housing) - too much external stress can result in the inability to reflect on one's internal process.

3) Pregnancy or breast feeding.

4) Disabling medical conditions, including but not limited to cardiovascular disease/untreated hypertension.

5) Disabling, unstable, or acute mental illness(es).

6) Addiction-related conditions (e.g. active alcohol withdrawal).

7) Active or historical diagnosis of any serious psychiatric disorders such as bipolar disorder, schizophrenia/psychotic disorders, paranoia, and personality disorders. This is because these individuals are at a higher risk of protracted destabilization. The guide should be especially vigilant in cases of borderline and narcissistic personality disorders, as they are hard to diagnose, tend to not respond well to many forms of treatment and can behave aggressively to anyone to attempts to help. The Maclean Screening Instrument for Borderline Personality Disorder can be used and is easily available. A score of 7 or more is considered a positive screen for this disorder.

Manual for Psychedelic Guides

8) Desperate, help-seeking/help-rejecting participants should be graciously avoided.

9) Over idealizes or demonizes current or past helpers/guides/therapists.

10) Severe trauma/dissociation.

11) High anxiety or panic attacks.

12) Poor or little emotional regulation.

13) Active or historical diagnosis of neurological disorders such as stroke, epilepsy, or serious brain injury, to minimize the risk of adverse events (e.g. inducing a seizure).

14) Moderate/advanced forms of dementia as these participants are not capable of giving informed consent.

15) Due to the theoretical risk of serotonin syndrome, participants currently using tricyclic antidepressants, serotonin-reuptake inhibitors (most standard antidepressants), MAOIs, and St. John's Wort, should be assessed carefully before participating in psychedelic sessions. The higher the dose of these medications the greater the concern. Individuals on mood stabilizers (e.g. lithium, valproic acid), or antipsychotic medications (e.g. haloperidol, risperidone) are likely to have been diagnosed with a serious mental illness, and thus should be considered with caution, as per #7. (Please see Appendix D for more information on pharmaceutical contraindications).

16) Suicidal or homicidal ideation.

17) Anger management problems.

18) Those who have parents (or first-degree relatives) with any psychotic or bipolar disorders, due to the increased risk of vulnerability to an underlying psychiatric disorder, via genetic/family history.

19) Participants who are a couple in conflict should be approached with caution. If a couple is treated together and one person decides to leave the relationship, there is the risk that the guide may be blamed.

20) Participants who have difficulty reflecting on their emotions, belief systems, etc., and taking responsibility for their actions, make the process of healing more challenging for both themselves and the guide.

21) A potential participant who has difficulty listening to the guide and taking in information during the preparatory session, will probably have similar difficulty listening during the session. Also guides should be aware of potential participants who have a strong attachment to their "story". Those who believe they know all their issues, and know what they need to work on, tend to have more difficult sessions. Being "humbled by the medicine" is part of the road to healing and growth.

22) Difficulty trusting the guide(s) during the preparatory sessions or negative transference toward one or both of the guides.

23) Negative attitude toward life in general /victim/ blaming mentality.

24) Little or no support network.

25) Partner/family unsupportive of psychedelic experiences.

Manual for Psychedelic Guides

26) Going through a difficult time (loss of loved one, divorce, loss of job, home, illness, etc.).

27) Cannot afford to follow through with several experiences if indicated. "Cost is an issue" may indicate how little they value this work or themselves especially when they clearly have money for other indulgences.

28) Doesn't accept responsibility for own mental health.

29) Desperation - *"you are my last hope!!!"*

30) Expectation that the experience will "fix" them.

31) Demonstrates resistance to healing.

32) Wanting to rush into the healing experience - pushing to book the experience or having an agenda.

33) Contacting the guide many times prior to intake and beyond - always with more questions/concerns.

34) Demonstrates a need to *drive* the process.

35) Controlling behavior/rigid mindset.

36) Lack of an "I" focus /seeking validation from others.

37) Is your friend or family member. Doing psychedelics with friends is completely different than guiding someone through a psychedelic experience. As a guide, there needs to be a healthy respect for boundaries. If the experience is challenging or intensely self-disclosing, this can complicate a friendship or family dynamic.

38) Provides few details during the intake assessment in some areas and you must subsequently probe to sufficiently assess.

Mark Haden

It's not that you can't work with people who have red flags, but they require very special attention, sometimes several initial sessions prior to treatment so you can get to know them and get a better idea of how they might respond to treatment. Trust is the main factor, so take the time to nurture trust and be authentic. Be ready to accept that for some people, psychedelic experiences may not be the best for them or you.

Each of these red flags comes with a risk to the participant and to the guide. Always focus on the safety and wellbeing of the participant, but don't forget about your own wellbeing. When you first start communicating with a participant, discuss with them the "rules of engagement". Also make it clear that you cannot accept them for the experience until after they do an intake and get to know them, and this "getting to know you" stage does not guarantee a psychedelic session.

Sometimes obtaining collateral assessment information from significant others (with full permission) is helpful to ensure accuracy.

Green Flags

As there are red flags, so there are green flags. The following is a list of issues that suggest that a participant will do particularly well during and after the psychedelic session.

1) Is experienced in talk therapy, groups, counselling, or coaching.

2) Is on their own journey of self-discovery (self-aware).

3) Expresses desire to do deep work.

4) Is aware of something blocking them (dark cloud).

Manual for Psychedelic Guides

5) Has a regular meditation/breathwork/yoga practice.

6) Open-minded.

7) Spiritually inclined/spiritual practices.

8) Ability to surrender and let go.

9) Already had positive psychedelic experiences.

10) Positive regard for psychedelic therapy

11) Enthusiastic about psychedelics - ready to heal.

12) Cost is not an issue.

13) Trusting/faith in you and the process.

14) Is prepared and ready for this work.

15) Doesn't have specific expectations, but is open to what happens.

16) Little pharmaceutical consumption/prescription drug use.

17) Displays an easy understanding and comfort with boundaries and non-sexual touch.

18) Has a good support network, close friends, partner or family who values this work.

19) Is well informed about psychedelics/therapy.

20) Appreciates the importance of integration and bodywork and has a plan to implement post-experience healing.

The more of these attributes you observe, the more likely there is to be a positive outcome.

Challenging Situations as a Result of Poor Screening

Some of the most challenging situations reported by psychedelic guides were a consequence of inadequate screening.

Examples are:

- Offering this service to one or both members of a couple, resulting in one of them deciding to end the relationship with the subsequent blaming of the guide. Asking the participant about potential reactions from family, friends and partners is important, as their complaints about new behaviours and new decisions can be problematic.

- Individuals with personality disorders can become very angry with the guide when they are not "cured". One indicator of a borderline personality disorder is a high level of desperation. This is often associated with an unwillingness to follow through on home-work assignments, especially ones that require self-reflection. Inability to show up (on time) for appointments is concerning. If every suggestion made results in a rebuttal, consider this to be a warning flag.

- Significant cardiovascular events during an ibogaine session and subsequent hospitalization.

Manual for Psychedelic Guides

Information Sharing and Clarification of Intent and Process

The following should be considered during the preparation process and covered across a few sessions:

1) Clarify the participant's intentions in detail. This is to assess the degree to which the participant is committed to the experience and will do the necessary work to maximize the chance of a positive outcome. In some cases, putting intentions in writing helps to clarify them.

2) The participant should be informed that she/he will be encouraged to "stay internal" as much as possible. This means they will spend the session lying down, with eyeshades on, listening to music with headphones. Describe the guiding process to the participant as being a non-directive support for the participant's Inner Healing Intelligence. The music is carefully chosen to assist the participant to relax and stay focused on the journey of healing. Conversation is possible but not encouraged. More conversation can be expected with the empathogens (e.g. MDMA, 3-MMC) while less conversation is appropriate with the classic psychedelics (e.g. LSD, psilocybin). There are many reasons for maintaining minimal or no conversation during the major part of the experience. One reason is that verbal communication, by definition, comes from the same place as ego, and personal identity. Furthermore, language inherently implies subject/object duality and separation. This tendency of language can hinder the goal of this work, which is to allow the manifestation for nondual experiences. Also, therapists who insist on communication/verbal therapy, can be disempowering for the participants' Inner Healing Intelligence.

3) Discuss the rule of "no sexual touching". Any sexual interaction between guides and participant is strictly prohibited. This agreement assures that neither the participant nor the guide will be exploited, while simultaneously fostering a safe environment

for offering physical comfort/healing during the treatment session.

4) Discuss the possibility of consensual physical contact with the participant in the form of nurturing touch or focused bodywork. The guide and participant should negotiate a comfortable physical distance between each other during the psychedelic-assisted sessions, and guides should remain attentive to any changes in the participant's comfort level with their degree of proximity.

5) If the guiding room/group space is available for viewing, showing this room to the participant in advance may reduce potential anxiety of the unknown.

6) Discuss the rule: "don't leave the space". The participant must understand the importance of this rule and agree to remain within the treatment area until completion of each session. At the end of the session it is the responsibility of the guide to assess the participant's emotional stability, and whether the effects of the medicine have sufficiently subsided, before permitting the participant to leave. This rule also applies to the guide as the participant should never be left alone. Participants who remove eyeshades and headphones and find themselves alone can find this traumatizing as this can produce or reignite an "attachment wound".

7) Discuss the rule: "no harm is done". The participant must agree to refrain from self-harm, harm to others, and harm to property. The participant agrees that she/he will comply with the guide's request to stop, if the guide determines that the participant is engaged in behaviour that is dangerous to themselves, others, or the space. The participant agrees that she/he will comply with the guide's requests, even if it may seem contrary to their best interests while in their altered state.

Manual for Psychedelic Guides

8) If there are two guides, at least one of them must be present in the room at all times. Except for occasional periods in which a guide may briefly leave the room (e.g. bathroom breaks), one at a time, both guides commit to remain with the participant throughout the duration of the psychedelic-assisted session, until the acute emotional and physical effects of the medicine have worn off.

9) The participant should be encouraged to create a "personal altar" where pictures of family, friends, personally or spiritually meaningful objects, and/or artwork can be placed on a table beside the bed/couch. Discuss with the participant what objects specifically they would like to bring to the session. Other than the altar, refrain from allowing the participant to change anything else in the room (e.g. furniture location, etc.). Focusing on the objects in the room can be a distraction from the inner work which is required. Guides should therefore encourage participants to let go and not try to control anything.

10) The participant should be encouraged to arrive at the experiential session with a relatively empty stomach. A very light breakfast (fruit, yogurt) is ideal. Dietary restrictions may be recommended, for a few days prior to the session, to reduce bowel motility during the session. Guides should suggest that the participant wear comfortable, loose-fitting clothing, with no make-up (which can get messy) or scent/perfume (which can be offensive or allergenic to some).

11) Practice a relaxation technique with the participant and instruct them to practice it at home for at least 10 minutes a day. The suggested relaxation technique is as follows:

    a) start by taking long slow deep breaths for 1-2 minutes

    b) focus on how this promotes general relaxation

    c) breathe relaxation into specific muscles

    d) be mindful of the sensations of breathing

    e) repeat the word "relax" or "peace" on the out breath

Inform the participant that practicing a relaxing breathing technique will be helpful as this will be the "life jacket" used in the event of turbulent experiences.

12) Discuss the importance of having someone who will support this integration process. This can be a private therapist, close family member, etc. If the participant believes that the experience alone will "fix" them, assure them that this is extremely unlikely and encourage them to consider the experience as just one step in a long journey.

13) Discuss the process of confidentiality and how this works for both the guide and the participant.

14) Suggest that the participant not make any sudden massive changes in their life (e.g. asking for a divorce, quitting a job) after the experience. Recommend waiting until the integration process has solidified before making any significant life-changing decisions.

15) Discuss the issue of emotional expression. Let the participant know that intense emotional expressions are welcome, if they feel it is right for them. Discuss in advance safe ways of expressing feelings. For example, screaming is fine, but screaming into a pillow is quieter. On the other hand, breaking things or hurting people as part of emotional expression cannot be part of the process.

16) Discuss the concept of "projection" as this process is intensified under the influence of a psychedelic. Describe how the

Manual for Psychedelic Guides

participant may see the guide as being mother / father / lover / abuser and project these past experiences onto the guide. Normalize this process and observe that you understand this process and periodically discussing this may be appropriate.

17) Establish the fact that individual psychedelic psychotherapy is NOT couples counselling. While sharing psychedelic space with a loving partner can help with bonding and resolving issues, this is not the agenda for any individual session. Participants should be aware that individuals who have been through a psychedelic experience can often make big life-changing decisions during the integration phase, which can include the ending of a relationship. The impacts of this should be discussed in advance with participants (and perhaps) their partners.

18) Discuss the importance of not having access to phones, computers, etc., to ensure an undisturbed journey. All electronic devices, belonging to both the participant and guide, should be left at home or turned off for the duration of the session.

19) Discuss how the participant is going to go home after the session. Driving themselves is not an option which should be considered. A car accident after an intense spiritual or meaningful experience makes the subsequent integration process challenging.

20) Be explicit that the healing is not "magic," and does not happen without active engagement in the integration process. The common images relating to the psychedelic mechanism, showing the formation of "new brain connections", can be problematic, as they can lead to a belief that taking a psychedelic is like surgery, where one "goes under" and then "emerges transformed," or the experience will be like taking their car into a garage to be fixed, and they don't need to be part of the process. Discuss the fact that psychedelics can offer insights which need to be combined with subsequent integration work to manifest

any sustained change. Those who believe that the experience itself will "rewire the brain," without their participation, are not ideal candidates for the psychedelic experience.

21) Fear of an unknown "monster" in the unconscious mind is common. Many people are afraid of their unknown selves. It is helpful to acknowledge this and observe that monsters tend to turn into dance partners when approached with curiosity and compassion.

22) Payment options for the service should be discussed and agreed to.

    Introduce the following concepts to the participant:

    - Taking a psychedelic medicine is like journeying in a canoe on a river. Your guide will always be with you, but you are the one paddling on the river of self-exploration. <u>See appendix A</u>.

    - You are not alone. A guide will be with you at all times. Your environment will be safe, and you will get all the support you need.

    - The medicine will open up a world of possibilities for you. Using focus and attention, you have the power to choose which parts of your experience you want to explore.

    - Go with the flow of the session. If you find yourself having a hard time, remember that the degree of suffering is often equal to the degree of resistance. Trust the process and let go.

    - If you see a door – open it. If you see stairs – go up.

Manual for Psychedelic Guides

- If you find yourself feeling fear, be curious about what is bringing this up - the fear is in you. It is better to face and explore the fear than to keep avoiding it.

- Remain aware of what is going on in your body and be curious about any physical sensations, pleasure or pain.

- When you find yourself experiencing turbulence, anxiety or getting agitated, use the relaxation technique that you have been practicing. The best way to approach this work is with inner stillness and focus, much like a meditation practice.

- Pay more attention to how you feel than what you think. Be wary of your "story" or what you think you know.

- Above all, elicit and maintain gratitude. Trust the medicine, trust the process, and trust your own Internal Healer.

Dosage

While there is limited consensus within the psychedelic treatment community on appropriate dosage, some observations are appropriate.

- An analysis of historical research, conducted in the 50's and 60's, indicates that 200-300 micrograms of LSD was an appropriate first dose. Above this dosage significant ego disorientation can occur.

- Current research with psilocybin commonly uses 20-30 milligrams of pure psilocybin, which is approximately equivalent to 4-5 grams of dried *Cubensis* mushrooms.

- 80-125 milligrams of MDMA have been shown to be effective in current PTSD treatment research.

Mark Haden

- 200-300 milligrams of 3-MMC is seen as being effective by some current therapists

- 5-10 milligrams of smoked/vaporized freebase 5-MeO-DMT is the range currently being used by some guides. More than this can produce prolonged disorientation.

Research has shown that if you are guiding multiple sessions, incremental increases in the dosage produce optimal results.

The above information is not intended to offer recommendations for specific dosages. This decision should be made jointly with the participant, in consultation with the most updated information sources available (e.g. the website Erowid, recent clinical research etc.).

Time requirements

The timing of the onset and the main effects of different psychedelics vary widely. There are psychedelics which last minutes (e.g. 5-MEO-DMT), a few hours (e.g. 2CB, 3-MMC), approx. 6 hours (e.g. psilocybin, MDMA), 8-10 hours (e.g. LSD) and 36 hours (i.e. ibogaine). While the duration of the experience itself is reliably predictable, it is much harder to predict how long a participant will need support after the experience. Individuals vary widely, in both the time required to metabolize, and time required to re-orient sufficiently to function normally. A good rule of thumb is that all psychedelic experiences should be given at least one full day to be experienced. Taking a psychedelic in the morning and having to function later in the day is usually a significant mistake.

Informed Consent Process

Informed consent is a process by which potential participants are given full information, regarding all the potential risks and benefits

Manual for Psychedelic Guides

of participating in the psychedelic experience. Potential participants are able to have questions or concerns answered, and then voluntarily sign the informed consent form which, as described below, details a specific list of the areas covered by the agreement.

The Areas Covered by the Informed Consent Form

The participant...

- agrees to participate in a guided psychedelic experience

- understands the risks and benefits involved

- agrees to participate in the process which has been discussed (e.g. stay in the space during the day of experience, to not be physically aggressive towards the guide(s) or damage the treatment room, to refrain from sexual behaviour)

- agrees to participate in the integration process after the experience

- understands the importance of confidentiality

- understands the process of information/documentation collection and destruction

- agrees to the payment amount and process

Confidentiality

The guide and the participant should discuss how information is collected, protected, shared and destroyed. This includes a discussion on protecting the identify of all involved, including other participants if the process occurs in a group setting. This discussion should encompass:

- How is information collected including all forms, case notes and recordings?

- What is the format of this information (e.g. paper, electronic)?

- Where is this information kept (e.g. personal computer, the cloud, locked filing cabinet)?

- How is this information protected (locks, passwords, encryptions)?

- How long will it be kept?

- How will this information be destroyed?

- Who else will have access to this information, now and in the future, and what are the circumstances that result in sharing this information?

- What is the expectation of the participant to keep confidentiality?

- What kind of information is shared in emails and social media?

Manual for Psychedelic Guides

Offering experiences incrementally

For those who would like to have a psychedelic experience for the first time, incremental journeys can be a way of learning to navigate this space without diving into the deep end of the psychedelic pool. Starting with breathwork where the participant is guided to breathe deeply and rapidly while listening to psychedelic music is a gentle start. Then moving to a short acting medicine (e.g. DMT or 5-MeO-DMT) followed by a medicine which is not disorienting (e.g. MDMA or 3-MMC) before taking the deep dive into a classical psychedelic experience (e.g. LSD or psilocybin) is a gradual way of learning to access and navigate the unconscious mind.

Another way is to incrementally increase the dose of a single medicine over a number of sessions (e.g. 100, 200 and 300 micrograms of LSD). With short acting psychedelics the incremental experiences may be offered during the same day. The community of guides offering 5-MeO-DMT describe this as offering a handshake (2 mg), hug (4 mg) and full embrace (8 mg).

Mark Haden

Guiding the Session

Number of Guides

Ideally, there should be two guides (a male and a female) present for all psychedelic treatment sessions. This allows for the participant to project different internal material (e.g. past issues with mother and father) differentially on each guide. The presence of two guides also maximizes the growth of the team as their skills evolve through conducting sessions and debriefs. Additionally, having two guides is preferable, with respect to the safety of the guides as well as the participant.

It is noteworthy that the original male + female co-therapist model is being questioned by some members of the community, to incorporate non-binary, transgendered and other members with non-traditional gender identities as part of the healing team. Ultimately, the goal is to equip the team to match the needs and preferences of the participant.

If two guides are not realistically possible, and there is only one guide available, then it is important to discuss how projection and/or transference works. Projection and transference are a common part of the process, as the participant projects their shifting, and often intense, emotional and psychological experiences onto the guides. This can include both male and female issues, and a wide variety of emotional responses to past relationships on the single guide. It is useful to discuss this in advance and let the participant know that the guides' gender should not get in the way of their varied projection/transference process.

Items Which Should Be Available

- Sheets (and spare sheets)
- Warm blankets

Manual for Psychedelic Guides

- Weighted blanket – which can feel safe and comforting
- Pillows
- Wet wipes, towels, gloves
- Bucket or solid plastic garbage can
- Spare – one size fits all – clean clothes
- Music system that includes both headphones and speakers
- Eyeshades
- Spiritual cards (e.g. Angel cards, Medicine Cards, Animal Spirit cards)
- Singing bowl or gong (which can be used to signify change)
- Juice and fruit
- Water
- Different sensory experiences – flavours, textures
- Fresh flowers (a rose is traditional)
- Light snack for after the session
- Art supplies
- Pen and paper
- A small table for the personal altar

Mark Haden

- Teddy bear – big enough to hug

Music

Music use can be used to direct the experience of those who are participating in a psychedelic experience. A number of multi-hour playlists should be prepared, with semi-standardized music sets. The sets can be progressive, starting with music that is relaxing at first, then moving into more active and emotionally evocative music, to finally end with quieter and more meditative music. The playlist can be changed as needed, to fit the general mood and flow of the session. It is important that at least one of the treatment team members be familiar with the music to support and reflect each stage of the participant's process. Participants should be told to let the music "wash over them" with the process described as a "healing sound bath", and to recognize that the music keeps changing. They are also welcome to ask for periods of silence, or even a change in music if a piece of music is distracting or doesn't fit well with their

Manual for Psychedelic Guides

process. However, they should be discouraged from expending attention to manage the music.

Some participants may want to bring their own music for the guide to incorporate into their psychedelic-assisted sessions. While this should generally be discouraged, in certain circumstances it may be appropriate. It is important to consider the reasons for the request to ensure that it serves to support and deepen the process, rather than to control or distract oneself from feelings that may be emerging. While some degree of flexibility regarding such requests is desirable, treatment teams should minimize participant involvement in music selection. Participants are encouraged to ask for anything they need to help them feel safe and supported in the therapeutic setting. However, this should be balanced by encouraging participants to allow the treatment team to attend to the physical details of the session, and to trust them, as much as possible to provide a safe and salutary setting. This is part of cultivating an attitude of surrender, trust, and receptivity in the participant, to support and nurture the natural unfolding of the therapeutic process guided by the Inner Healing Intelligence. If any issues arise, participants should be asked to notice any tendency they may have to want to control the music or other aspects of the setting, and to consider exploring this tendency as part of their inner process, rather than to act on it externally.

Songs with no recognizable lyrics are preferable, as identifiable words can be distracting for the participant. Any music that is easily associated with a specific religious or spiritual tradition is discouraged, as this can create attachments and projections. Therefore, it is preferable to exclude ayahuasca *icaros*, Buddhist chants, or Hindu and Christian songs. Specific music suggestions can be found in Appendix C.

As the Participant Arrives for the Session

When the participant arrives, welcome them and conduct a quick "check-in". Notice if the participant is intoxicated on other substances. If yes, do not continue with the experience. Ask about recent food consumption, as too much food in the stomach can slow the process and cause vomiting during the experience. Invite the participant to use the washroom before the session begins, as "starting on empty" is helpful to avoid any future distraction.

Beginning of the Psychedelic Session

The following topics should be covered (in the order below) after the participant is comfortably sitting up on the bed and before the participant ingests the medicine. Although these topics should have been discussed in detail during the preparatory sessions, it is important to discuss them again at the beginning of the psychedelic session. Simply stating the points to the participant is discouraged. Instead, asking them to explore their understanding of each point is preferable.

1) Ask the participant about their intentions for this specific session. But be aware that the response may come from a place of "story" and ego. If a discussion ensues, encourage the participant to set their intentions around relaxing, staying present, while allowing feelings and expressions to emerge. It can be helpful to set the unstructured goal of authentically paying attention and remaining open to all experiences.

2) Ask the participant about their understanding of the rule: "no sexual touching". Any sexual behaviour between the guides and the participant is unethical and explicitly prohibited. This agreement assures the participant that her/his heightened vulnerability will not be exploited, while simultaneously fostering a safe environment for offering any physical comfort during the treatment session.

3) Ask the participant about their understanding of the possibility of physical contact in the form of nurturing touch or focused bodywork. The guide and participant should negotiate a comfortable physical distance between themselves during the

Manual for Psychedelic Guides

experiential sessions. The guide should remain attentive to any possible changes in the participant's level of comfort with their degree of physical proximity.

4) Ask the participant about their understanding of the rule: "don't leave the space". The participant must agree that she/he will remain within the treatment area until completion of each session. At the end of the session, it is the responsibility of the treatment team to assess the participant's emotional stability, and ensure that the effects of the psychedelic medication have sufficiently subsided, before permitting the participant to leave. Also discuss the fact that this rule applies to the guide, who will not leave the participant alone.

5) Ask the participant about their understanding of the rule: "no harm is done". The participant must agree to refrain from self-harm, harm to others, and/or harm to property. The participant must agree that she/he will comply with the guides' request to stop, if the guide determines that the participant is engaged in behaviour that is dangerous to themselves, to others, or to the space.

6) Mention to the participant that at least one of the members of the guide team will be present in the room, at all times, throughout the entire treatment session. Other than occasional periods when a guide may briefly leave the room, one at a time, both treatment team members commit to remaining in the room with the participant throughout the duration of the treatment session, until the acute emotional and physical effects of the psychedelic have worn off. If there is only one guide for the treatment session, the fact that this person may need to be briefly absent should be discussed with the participant.

7) Discuss the "bathroom process" (see details below).

8) Inform the participant that the goal is to "stay internal" as much as possible. This means they are encouraged to spend the

session lying down, with eyeshades on, listening to music through headphones, and focusing on their internal processes. Nonetheless, the participant may choose to take the eyeshades and/or headphones off at any time. The participant also has the option to request periods of silence, and the guides have the option to curate the music to fit the unfolding experience. Guides should aim to use the music to support the experience, without being intrusive.

9) Encourage the participant to create a "personal altar" on a table beside the bed, where pictures of family, friends, meaningful or spiritual objects, or works of art can be placed.

10) Participants can be encouraged to fully express themselves vocally during the session through laughing, crying, toning, glossolalia, etc., with the understanding that they need not communicate anything specific via language. This can assist in the exploration of energetic states and experiences, without the need to "explain" or "describe" anything to anyone in the moment of the experience.

11) Introduce the analogy of the canyon river canoe trip – see suggested full text – appendix A.

12) Explain the next steps:

   A. The participant will take the medicine.

   B. The guide will offer a guided meditation and breathing exercise.

   C. The treatment team will become silent and the music will guide the experience.

   D. The participant is encouraged to "stay internal" as much as possible.

Manual for Psychedelic Guides

13) Give the medicine to the participant and observe the previously agreed upon dose of medication is ingested by the participant.

14) Offer a guided relaxation experience. Specifically, ask the participant if they would like a guided meditation to help in the process of relaxing. If the response is "yes", a guide should talk slowly and peacefully through a guided meditation. See example in appendix B.

16) Ask the participant to put the headphones and eyeshades on, and then start the music playlist.

17) Notice the breathing of the participant. Try and match your breathing rates to create and then maintain your feelings of connection. Meditate to slow your thoughts and build your own awareness of your surroundings. It can be challenging for the guide to maintain presence when the participant is "internal". As the participant can remove the eyeshades at any time, it is important to be there for them when they "resurface". The participant will often know if the guide is distracted or not, and so matching breathing rates and continuing meditation are useful techniques for staying focused on the participant.

Mark Haden

In the end, some of your greatest pains become your greatest strengths.

- Drew Barrymore

Manual for Psychedelic Guides

Psychedelic Group Experiences

In indigenous communities, psychedelics have traditionally been offered in the context of a group experience. Current researchers have generally chosen to provide this experience to one participant at a time. This may change over time however, as groups have a number of advantages.

1) Groups are more efficient and therefore the cost per person is lower, making the experience more accessible.

2) Taking a psychedelic in a group can be a highly bonding experience for the participants. This can enhance treatment effectiveness for conditions like depression, which tends to be an isolating experience.

3) Groups can add a safety factor to the experience, as guides who have "boundary challenges" will be less likely to intrude on participants if there are many witnesses.

When offering the psychedelic experience in a group context, it is best to conduct the screening and assessment process individually. The participant is introduced to the group if they pass the screening, after which group norms are established and relationships between the participants develop. All the processes related to establishing and running a psychotherapy group apply when working with psychedelics, as well. Ideally, the group should develop their own communication rules around issues of confidentiality, how to talk in a group, how to listen, managing time, interruptions, giving advice to other participants, empathy, etc. Participants need to develop these skills within both psychedelic experience groups (where internal experiences are predominant) and integration groups (where talking is normal).

Mark Haden

Helping members understand the importance of not intruding on others during the experiences is essential. Therefore, issues like limiting eye contact in group should be discussed. Dim lighting during the experience tends to reduce eye contact and assists people to focus inwardly on themselves, not on others.

Toileting should also be discussed as participants may need assistance walking.

The roles of the different guides should be clarified, as some guides may be specialized (e.g. to offer music), while others may offer psychological support.

After a participant has been screened and assessed, as appropriate, most of the rest of the work can happen in the group. The preparation, psychedelic experiences, debrief, and follow-up can all be done in group, with a few exceptions.

While groups can offer advantages in both efficiency and effectiveness, groups also have disadvantages. Unwanted connections between participants may be more difficult to regulate. Some connections can result in unhealthy experiences and the reduced confidentiality can result in undesirable information sharing outside the group, in spite of confidentiality agreements. Groups generally work better if everyone in the group perceives the other members as being peers.

Manual for Psychedelic Guides

Dealing with Specific Behaviours

Talking During the Beginning and Middle of the Session

Generally, during the "ascent" stage and "peak" stage, the participant is encouraged to "stay internal" and lie down with the eyeshades and headphones. However, if the participant insists on talking, then the goal of the guiding team is to offer empathetic presence and listening, non-directive communication, and support for the participant's Inner Healing Intelligence. Empathetic presence entails providing a non-judgmental environment, which offers psychological permission to talk openly and honestly. It requires listening beneath and beyond the spoken words for deeper meanings, acknowledging the other's suffering or joy, and validating the participant's feelings. The goal of communication during the beginning and middle of the session is to provide minimal responses, which communicates an empathetic presence, and therefore allows the participant to experience connection to the guides.

Moving Around the Room

While the goal is to encourage the participant to "stay internal" and remain lying down, if the participant insists on moving around the room, a guide can draw their attention to various parts of the room that are inspirational or beautiful. For example, a guide can offer a flower or a deck of "animal spirit" cards, and then allow the participant to reflect on the meaning of the card drawn.

Moving Unpredictably

If the participant's movements are unpredictable, and could result in an injury, the guide should be ready to quickly move a pillow to protect a participant's head (or other body part) from any hard surfaces. When working with a fast-acting and dramatically powerful medicine, such as 5-MeO-DMT, for example, it is best to have the participant situate themselves on a bed or mattress before consumption. Once the medicine has been consumed, the participant can lie back, trusting that they will not hit their head. This allows for full surrender to the experience without last-moment concerns of physical safety.

Asking the Guide Personal Questions

If the guide is asked personal questions, the goal is to demonstrate personal integrity and provide an honest answer, but not to let the personal material of the guide intrude on the experience of the participant. For example, if asked "why do you do this work?" an appropriate answer could be "I have found altered states of consciousness to be very helpful in my own life and I am honoured to have the opportunity to support deep healing journeys for others – I am fascinated by the experience of being human and I get to celebrate all human experiences during these sessions – thank you for trusting me to guide you", or "Today is about you and your experience, we can talk more about me and my experiences later". Before responding to personal questions, it is helpful to consider whether the self-disclosure relates to the participant's experience and helps them connect to the guide. Integrity with minimum self-disclosure is the goal.

Becoming Increasingly Anxious and Agitated

The best response to a participant's anxiety is to first demonstrate a calm, compassionate presence. Holding the participant's hand, and making gentle statements such as the following can be useful: "trust the medicine" or "trust your own Internal Healer to show you what you need to see" or "take long slow deep breaths" or "everything is alright" or "you're doing great, this is all part of the process". Notice how the person is breathing (e.g. chest breathing, stomach breathing, nose, mouth) and suggest that they breath in a different way. Such a change of focus is helpful and can be used to slow down the breath and make the feelings more manageable. Be aware of the different yogic breathing exercise and

Manual for Psychedelic Guides

use as appropriate. Sometimes, body work, where you encourage the participant to move from the bed to the carpet on the floor and offer pressure point massage, is a way of refocusing the participant. Pressure point massage is especially useful in areas of bodily pain or discomfort. You can start this process by asking "where do you feel this most strongly in your body?" Other times it may be appropriate to change the music to help the participant to refocus. A carefully chosen poem or insightful text can also help. For example:

> *"Under the hard there is fear,*
> *Under the fear is sadness.*
> *In the sadness is softness.*
> *In the softness is the vast open space."*

Offering something to stimulate other senses can be helpful. A shot of a strong ginger or lime flavoured beverage, or something to chew, or suck on, can help refocus. Different sounds can be also created; for example, a rattle, bell, gong or chime, to provide focus and soothe. Generally, anxiety is not a "bad" experience, and the goal is to help the participant stay with the experience until their Inner Healing Intelligence changes the experience.

Only in extremely rare circumstances, when safety is an issue, and if deemed appropriate by the guide or attending physician as a very last resort, the participant may be offered a medication (i.e. a benzodiazepine), to help them relax.

If the Participant is Extremely Emotional

Intense emotional responses are not uncommon during psychedelic healing experiences, in response to the participant's internal turbulence/trauma. A calm, compassionate presence is the preferred therapeutic modality, as this helps participants manage their own anxiety. The main goal for the guide is to stay calm and focused and to maintain a compassionate presence, understanding that the participant's Inner Healing Intelligence is guiding this intense emotional release, and that it is an important part of the participant's healing journey. Reflective listening is an important skill so that the participant feels understood, which is an important aspect of psychological safety. If this process is a triggering experience for the guide, it will be important to discuss it at the post-session debrief with colleagues. Participants, generally, are very "in tune" with guides' emotions. As such, it is paramount for the guides to stay calm in the presence of emotional turbulence. The overall approach is to contain, not restrain. Sometimes words are not the best mode of communication and music is the preferred vehicle of influence. As mentioned above, changing the music can have a dramatic effect on the mood of the experience. Watch the environment closely if intense emotions are expressed as hitting one's head on a hard surface can be problematic during this time.

Trying to Leave the Space

It is useful to have a plan in advance to manage a participant who wants to leave the space. Memorize a repetitive statement, which the guide repeats as many times as is necessary, to ask the participant to stay in the space. The statement should be both reflective/empathetic, while simultaneously setting a boundary. For example: "I understand that you want to leave, but this room is a safe space, and we are both going to stay here and deal with this experience together," or, "I understand you feel afraid. Together we will deal with this, and together we are going to stay in this room where it is safe". A planned distraction can be helpful, for example, saying, "I would like to show you something", and then pulling out a deck of spiritual cards, or changing the music to create a different environment.

Going to the Bathroom

The participant may be unsteady on their feet and may need help walking to the bathroom. The guide should offer their arm for the participant to hold as they walk to the bathroom. Another alternative is that the participant rests their hands on the guide's shoulders and they both walk – facing the same direction – with the

Manual for Psychedelic Guides

participant "in tow". Check to make sure there is adequate, immediately available toilet paper and the roll (if it is new) has already been started. As the participant goes inside the bathroom, the guide closes the door behind them and lets them know that they will wait outside for them, and will be there to assist them back to the treatment room, when they are finished. The guide should be able to access the washroom (by way of opening the locked door or by suggesting to the participant not lock the door) in the event of an emergency. If the participant takes too long in the bathroom, the guide should inform the participant, strongly if necessary, that it is time to return to the experience room.

Vomiting

Some participants will vomit during the psychedelic experience (especially when using Ayahuasca or with those who are experienced with Ayahuasca and have linked the psychedelic experience with purging). Having a bucket (or empty plastic trash can) available is important. Being supportive, without encouraging or discouraging the purge process, is the goal. Having clean towels, wipes, surgical gloves, sealable plastic bags, etc. to quickly clean up the participant or the bed is important.

Urine or Bowel Release

Bladder and bowel accidents are more common with Ayahuasca, but can happen with any psychedelic medicine. Having the following available is useful: accident proof bed cover, wet wipes, towels, gloves and garbage bags (to control odor). Having some "one size fits all" clothes can also be useful, if the participant's clothes get soiled. Discussing how to handle this rare, but unpleasant, possibility in advance can be helpful.

Fire Alarm or Earthquake

In the event of a fire alarm or an emergency, where the participant and guides are required to leave the space, the goal is to weave this experience into the overall process. Both guides should escort the participant out of the building, minimizing contact with other people, and then finding a space that is as quiet and natural as possible. Walking to a local park and focusing on the beautiful environment is the ideal response.

Cuddling

Occasionally, cuddling a participant may be appropriate. For example, if participants are re-working a childhood parental bonding deficit, cuddling could provide support to process the emotions. It is important to offer this experience without any sexual implications and in response to a participant invitation. Cuddling can occur with the participants back to the guides front. The two could be lying side by side or partially sitting up. A third option is for the participant to be lying on the bed facing up and the guide to have their knees on the floor and offering a "torso only" hug. If cuddling occurs during the session, addressing it before subsequent sessions is important. In retrospect, some participants can feel embarrassed by this, and it is important to explain how this can be part of the healing experience and is not a sexual process.

Sexual behaviour

In spite of a prior discussion stating that there will be "no sexual touching" sometimes participants have sexual experiences. This issue is more likely with MDMA than other psychedelics. The appropriate response is to both continue to be supportive and be open while maintaining professional boundaries AND to not shame the participant. It is helpful to offer the message that "this is your projection" and has nothing to do with me (the guide) and I will help you to work with your projection in a way that keeps our "no sexual touching" agreement. Gracious humor can be one method of diffusing this challenging situation. Debriefing these kind of

Manual for Psychedelic Guides

experiences with other staff is important as responding appropriately to this behaviour can be challenging.

Spiritual Bypass

There are those in the psychedelic therapeutic community who believe that if a participant has a spiritual experience, they can be using this experience to avoid reflecting on self. This is described as being a "spiritual bypass" and seen as being undesirable as it means that the participant is unwilling to deal directly with their unconscious psychological traumas etc., and therefore will not reap the healing benefits which psychedelics can offer. This is in contrast to the research which observes that a profound mystical experience is often highly correlated with positive treatment outcomes. This belief also contrasts with the concept of the Inner Healing Intelligence which believes that participant's internal healer knows the appropriate path for optimal healing, and both reflection on self and mystical experiences are helpful in the healing process.

Mark Haden

During the Last Part of the Session

As the medicine subsides in the last two hours of a session, the participant may want to talk. At this stage, instead of continuing to encourage the participant to "stay internal", allow for a discussion that is empathetic and "non-directive".

The essence of what constitutes "non-directive" communication is in the timing of interventions. More active engagement under appropriate circumstances is not discouraged. In fact, there are occasions when failure to offer guidance in a sensitive way would be as problematic as being overly directive. What is essential is that the pace of the session allows for the participant's own process to unfold spontaneously, and that the guides allow ample time for this unfolding before offering any direction. For example, if a participant is feeling stuck, the initial approach should be to encourage them to feel this experience, trusting that the Inner Healing Intelligence will guide their response. When the guide offers direction, it should be done in the spirit of compassionate, collaborative inquiry and invitation, leaving the choice up to the individual. Within the context of a session where the participant's Inner Healing Intelligence has taken the overall lead, offering directions at specific times is entirely compatible with the definition of a non-directive approach.

Non-directive communication also uses invitation rather than direction. For example:

- "I encourage you to …"

- "This might be a good time to …"

- Instead of saying "breathe" (which is a directive statement) say "breathing" as this is suggestive and tracks the participants experience.

Manual for Psychedelic Guides

- Reflecting back to the participant what they are saying in order to continue conversation, without being directive.

- Working with the participant's Inner Healing Intelligence to resolve the expression of painful feelings

- "We're right here with you, focus on your breath, and stay with it as much as you can. We know this is difficult, but we also know from experience that this is an important part of the healing. Fully experiencing and expressing the feelings, moving through it instead of away from it is the way to really heal it."

With a combination of empathetic listening, questions, and observations, the guides facilitate two complementary aspects of processing these challenging experiences. On the one hand, helping participants with facing (and even amplifying) the experience, in order to allow the spontaneous unfolding of the healing process.

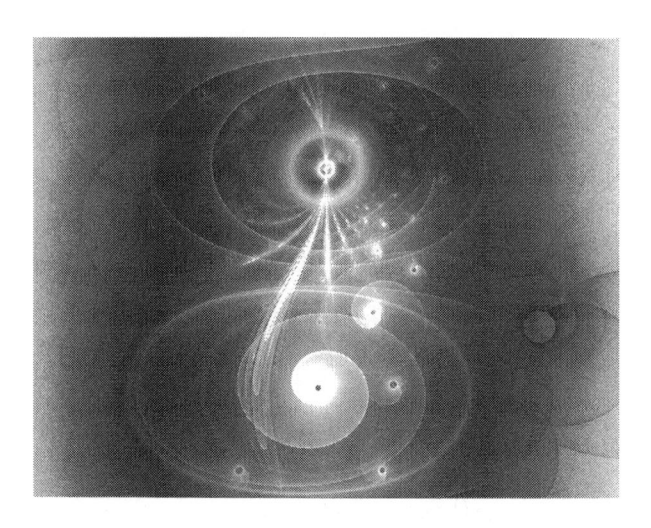

Mark Haden

Bringing Resolution to Turbulence at the Ending of a Session

When a participant's emotional distress persists into the end of the session, and they are not able to process and spontaneously move through something difficult, the following steps may be helpful. In most cases, these steps should be taken sequentially, proceeding to the next step only if necessary. There are two fundamental approaches to consider as you either work to "go deeper and resolve" or "move away and move on".

1. When trying to "move on" sometimes simple distraction works. Refocusing on something else can sometimes be helpful. Changing the music, getting up and moving or opening curtains to look outside can refocus attention.

2. Refocusing from emotional turbulence to sensations in the body can also be helpful. Ask: "What are you aware of in your body?" Making the link to somatic sensations and then suggesting to them to "breathe into that area and allow your experience to unfold" may be helpful. Applying a light pressure from the guide's hand to the area of sensation or pain, can help resolve the issue.

3. Sometimes resolution is achieved by diving more deeply into the experience. One option is to encourage the participant to "use your breath to help you stay as present as you can with this experience. Go inside to allow your Inner Healing Intelligence to work with this".

4. Sometimes shifting to a discussion is helpful. Ask "Is there any specific content (images, memories, or thoughts) coming up with these feelings?" If so, the guide may encourage discussion and the process of explaining the situation can distract from the actual experience. The opportunity itself, to put the experience into words, may be therapeutic.

Manual for Psychedelic Guides

5. After this period of talking, and periodically throughout the session as well, encourage the participant to "go back inside", to focus on her/his own inner experience.

6. Sometimes emotional turbulence can be a result of low blood sugar and offering fruit juice and healthy food can help to both distract and bring back physical balance.

Mark Haden

Concluding the Session

Careful consideration needs to be given to the ending a psychedelic session. A close bond has probably been formed between the guide and the participant and an abrupt ending can reopen a historical "attachment wound" or create new emotional distress. Rituals can be helpful in honouring the transition away from the psychedelic experience, and openly discussing how this transition feels is also important. The general principle is that "it is not over until it is over for everyone". This means that the guide needs to continue to offer support/presence until the participant clearly states they are ready for the transition to "normal". In order to bring closure, it is helpful to ask the participant if they would be willing to reflect on their initial intention, and discuss any conclusions they might have reached, as they reflect back on the experience. The goal here is to clarify and solidify the lessons that have been learned.

It can be useful in the integration process to ask the participant to write a paragraph about the experience, giving them the choice to do this immediately after the session, or at home that same evening, to be returned to the guide the next day for discussion during the first integration session.

Manual for Psychedelic Guides

Post-Session Debrief

As guides often work in pairs, they both have a responsibility to actively work on their relationship with each other. This is important because an easy flow of information will maximize the learning for both guides. Furthermore, rectifying any latent issues is crucial as any unresolved conflicts between the guides will probably be perceived by the participant, and will hinder the effectiveness of the session. Therefore, guiding partners need to debrief after all sessions and discuss in advance how they will conduct the debriefing sessions. Talking about the balance between both their voices, being mindful of any perceived interruptions by one guide over the other, preparing for any triggering or countertransference issues is important. Debriefing the debrief is also important – the question "how was this process for you?", is important in order to keep communication open.

Behaviours to Avoid

A skillful guide will never:

- Tell a participant who they are.

- Insist on asking questions.

- Believe their insights and guidance are more useful than the participant's own Inner Healing Intelligence.

- Believe that it is useful to "help dissolve the participant's ego".

- Be intrusive to the participant's process because they know better.

- Touch in a way that is not welcomed by the participant.

- Interrupt the other guide.

- Dominate the session.

- Demonstrate unclear professional or personal boundaries.

- Leave a participant before the participant feels ready to end the session.

Offer What You Have

It is important to have a sufficient understanding of psychedelics so that you can confidently provide clear answers to the participant's questions. Be willing to acknowledge that you don't know if you are not confident of an answer.

Manual for Psychedelic Guides

Integration

Don't spend all of your time trying to FIND yourself. Spend your time CREATING yourself into a person that you'll be proud of.

- Sonya Parker

Sometimes participants feel anxiety, confusion and disorientation (or crazy) for a period of time (a few days or occasionally weeks) after an intense psychedelic experience. Generally, this is not a long-term concern if it is managed skillfully. The integration process starts the day after the experience and can continue for as many sessions as needed to facilitate the integration process. If the guide is also a therapist, any specific therapeutic techniques they possess are appropriate during the integration stage, as long as the Inner Healing Intelligence of the participant is also continually engaged. Integration is facilitated with detailed memories of what occurred during the psychedelic experience. Listening to any audio recordings of the session, or to the same music tracks the next day and journaling during this process assists in the recall process.

The Goals of the Integration Process are:

1) To reduce negative experiences/feelings after the psychedelic experience.

2) To work on the insights gained during the experience.

3) To make positive external (e.g. find a better job) or internal (e.g. shifting to more constructive thought patterns) or social (e.g. relationship) changes.

4) To maintain a positive connection with the guide.

5) To enhance existing (and build new) connections with others who are supportive of healthy emotional and behaviour changes.

The Initial Process of Integration:

1) Start with the general question "How are you doing"?

2) Ask the participant about both the positive and challenging aspects of the treatment session.

3) Discuss the participant's intentions (as discussed in the preparation process).

4) Ask about their home environment or any significant social contacts they had after the experience. Interactions with others (e.g. partner, family or friends) who are not supportive, can be problematic to the process of integration. Reflecting on these conversations from a healing perspective can be useful.

5) If the participant reports increased anxiety, distress or disorientation, explain to them that this is a common and natural part of the healing process. Perhaps use the analogy of a physical bruise and the swelling which occurs with physical trauma, which are both painful and distressing, but are an inevitable part of the natural cycle of healing. Explain to them that the process of dealing with this is to focus on the basics such as: good diet, gentle exercise, talking about underlying issues with a counsellor or close friend, good sleep hygiene, avoiding alcohol/caffeine/non-prescription drugs, and social support.

6) Do a detailed examination of "lessons learned" from the treatment experience.

Manual for Psychedelic Guides

7) Ask the participant about their plan for integration and how they intend on acting on the insights gained during the experience.

8) Discuss with them how the real work is just beginning and the "lessons learned" are quickly unlearned if we do not work at integrating our thoughts/behaviours/feelings/relationships. During the psychedelic experience, one becomes aware of the (often unhealthy) unconscious thought loops, and emotional reactions that can drive seemingly automatic behaviour patterns. The challenge of integration is to form new, healthy conscious thought loops which are practiced repetitively until they drop into the unconscious mind and then become automatic positive thought loops. The old thought loops will not completely disappear immediately, but need to be slowly allowed to become dormant, by continuously strengthening the new thought loops. Unconscious thought loops are like biceps – the more you exercise them, the stronger they get. Integration is all about building and repeatedly exercising healthy new internal processes. Changing behaviours that are driven by unconscious thought loops is often uncomfortable at first, and support and understanding is needed in order to persist in walking this path of healing.

9) Discuss how the participant can improve their existing relationships with family, friends and their community, and build new connections which support the positive emotional and behavioural changes that they are processing.

10) Ask for feedback to help improve the guiding process in the future:

- How was the session guide?

- How was the room/music/space?

- Did you feel safe?

- Was the preparation adequate?

- Can you offer any feedback to help improve the experience in the future?

Integration Over Time

The process of integration can be short or may take many years. The goal is to make the psychological, social, emotional, environmental or physical changes that are needed to improve the quality of the participant's life. This process could be supported by the psychedelic guides themselves. Or it could be facilitated by an external therapist, counsellor, friend or family member. The main message should be that psychedelics by themselves are not a cure. While these carefully structured psychedelic experiences can result in profound insights, they still need to be acted on to make long-term changes in life.

Life is a journey, not a destination.

- Ralph Waldo Emerson

Manual for Psychedelic Guides

Code of Ethics

Both the participant and guides take on special responsibilities as they cultivate a unique relationship. As psychedelic experiences can be very powerful, they can be transformative, but also there can be risks. To manage these risks, the following code of ethics can offer guidance:

Integrity

Guides shall strive to be aware of how their own belief systems, values, needs, and limitations affect their work, and seek counsel from other guides, or a supervisor, when experiencing conflict regarding these aspects of their identity.

Competence

Guides participate only when they are qualified through personal experience, training, and education. This includes thorough knowledge of the set and setting, and deep understanding of the unique effects of each psychedelic substance. They should also demonstrate skillfulness in the non-directive therapeutic approach and other principles of a psychedelic guidance, while maintaining vigilant awareness of the participant's needs.

Health and Safety

Guides shall make reasonable preparations to protect and promote the health and safety of each participant, while maintaining their own health and safety as well. This includes recognizing that there may be periods in which the participant may be sensitive or vulnerable. Managing these periods require forethought in relation to safeguarding the setting, as well as the set. Make yourself aware of the actions to take if there is a natural disaster (e.g. earthquake), significant problem with the building/space (e.g., fire, flood), or a medical or any other emergency.

Mark Haden

Healthy Boundaries

Both participants and guides shall establish and honour honest communication, trust, rapport, and confidentiality. A discussion about healthy boundaries should also be a part of this process. Any limits on the behaviours of participants and guides are to be made clear and agreed upon before any session. Guides shall be aware of possible transference, countertransference, projection, power differential, and other aspects related to participant-guide relationship and also take responsibility for maintaining professional ethical boundaries at all times. While the alliance-building aspect of psychedelics can be very helpful in facilitating the treatment process, it can also be problematic. If guides (and participants) cross the line and develop a personal or sexual relationship, it can be destructive for the healing process and problematic for the entire community of professionals who are involved with this work. Setting clear boundaries is helpful to maintain a professional relationship. The following can be helpful:

- Only see a participant in your office or guiding space – keep your personal space separate.

- Predetermine about how much time you will spend with the participant.

- If two guides work together, outline a mutual agreement that a guide will never spend (significant) time alone with the participant.

- Be aware of borderline and other personality disorders, as these can manifest as urgent requests for help and result in close association.

- Decline post treatment requests for any social contact from the participant.

Manual for Psychedelic Guides

- Include "counter transference" as a recurring agenda item in discussions with your guiding partner/team, where all emotional responses to the participants are candidly discussed. Notice any internal hesitation to share an emotional response with a team member, as that is the first clue that a boundary has been (or is about to be) crossed. In order to maintain integrity, take a deep breath and talk about this emotion.

Compassion Fatigue

Guides are accountable for knowing symptoms of compassion fatigue, and for taking measures, on a personal basis, to prevent its negative effects. Guides strive to promote a centered, joyful and professional presence. It is important for the guide to take responsibility of knowing when they need a break from their healing practice, to prevent burn-out. This work can be difficult and draining and work-life balance is important to remain effective. On the airplane we are told to put on our own oxygen masks first, and only then help others. This analogy applies here as well, as our own lives have to be in balance for us to be able to effectively help others.

Being a Psychedelic Guide

Just like psychedelic experiences are not for everyone, being a psychedelic guide is also not for everyone. There are significant challenges and rewards for those who choose to provide this service. The challenges include boredom (it is hard to sit for many hours in silence), fear (unpredictable behaviour is not uncommon), physical inactivity (sitting can be hard on the body) and dealing with both positive and negative projections from the participant. The rewards are also significant as it is indeed a huge honour to participate in what is often the most meaningful, transformative or spiritual experience of a participant's life.

Mark Haden

The best way to find yourself is to lose yourself in the service of others.

- *Mohandas Karamchand Gandhi*

Ongoing Training

Becoming a psychedelic guide is a process which requires ongoing training, deep reflection, and skillful supervision. Experiential training like Holotropic breathwork, individual or group psychotherapy, inner exploration retreats, and meditation, are all recommended to help build the skills, knowledge and personal insights needed to be effective, with both participants and colleagues. One consistent goal is to develop a deep awareness of one's own "projections" and "unconscious filters", as these can be problematic in work with participants, as well as in relationships with others. For example, a guide with a history of personal trauma who "projects" this trauma on participants, may be unable to match the experience of the participant or may alienate their colleagues. Understanding and being able to discuss transference and counter transference issues is important, as these issues are considerably amplified when working with psychedelics.

Manual for Psychedelic Guides

Being a Functional Member of a Team

Often guides work in teams and offer the psychedelic experience in couples – most commonly – male and female. It is essential for guides to have utmost trust in the entire process – in their own skills, their team, the medicine, and the participants' innate healing capacity. Equally important is the cohesiveness of the team as a whole. While every guide should resonate with whomever they are paired with, they need to also be aware and supportive of the whole team, while communicating openly with all members. Members of a guiding team who are paired together to co-facilitate a psychedelic session should spend time together, with the intention of developing a trusting interpersonal relationship where open communication is possible. This relationship fosters learning for both guides, and allows for a constructive, healthy debrief at the end of the session. A skilled guide understands the larger context of their work, as psychedelic work requires many people with diverse backgrounds and skills. Forging and maintaining constructive relationships with other team members is rarely easy and requires specific intention, time and energy, tolerance, respect for the skills of others, self-disclosure and trust.

Mark Haden

Future psychedelic research/self-guiding.

While research today focuses on the treatment of specific diagnoses, a review of experiences reported on the internet allows for speculation regarding possible future research options beyond the restrictions of the DSM (Diagnostic and Statistical Manual). Self-guided experiences with the goal of enhancement of relationships is just one example that shows promise for significant change. The book; Love Drugs: The Chemical Future of Relationships [49], explores how many substances including psychedelics can increase or decrease sexual functioning and pleasure, feelings of connection and intimacy, reflection, self-disclosure and empathy. As many websites have "trip reports", it can be observed that different psychedelics (and different dosages) offer couples a wide variety of different possible experiences. For example, sexual experiences are reported to be enhanced with MDMA or a combination of MDMA (100 mg) and LSD (50 mcg). This combination is popular enough to have the term "Candy Flip" coined. MDMA can enhance the experience of love and increase physical connections beyond just the sexual context. An empathogenic medicine which has been used in therapy is 3-MMC (3-Methyl methcathinone). Therapists like the fact that this medicine is less coloured by the emotion of love and is less physical than MDMA, hence ideal for many different types of talk therapy or specifically, conflict resolution. Couples who take a classic psychedelic (e.g. LSD or psilocybin) and eye gaze in silence for extended periods of time report increased connections. Even if there is no physical connection or conversation during a shared psychedelic experience (e.g. ayahuasca ceremony), the post session debrief can be a highly bonding experience.

Other avenues of potential future research include not just connections with loved ones, but using psychedelics to build connections with individuals who we perceive as different from ourselves. Connections with nature and the environment can also be

Manual for Psychedelic Guides

enhanced, and exploring the nuances of these changes could benefit us all. Exploring how psychedelics can help us develop our spirituality and understanding of the universe as a whole also has significant promise for a variety of avenues of research. Hopefully researchers in the future will be able to move beyond treatment for specific diagnoses and move into larger questions regarding our individual, societal and collective health and spirituality.

The integration of the psychedelic experience into existing and new spiritual / religious structures and traditions will be important to observe. As the setting of the psychedelic experience is vital and churches often offer beautiful structures the opportunity to infuse existing traditions with profound experiences may be compelling to religious leaders seeking to bolster congregations.

Conclusion

Being a psychedelic guide is not for everyone as it requires a significant commitment of time, training, energy, focus and can be extremely difficult during times of intensity. At this time there is not yet a professional designation with College oversight of those who offer psychedelic guiding services for payment and treatment of psychiatric/psychological conditions. It is predictable that this skill set will be formalized in the future, and designated professional training programs will be developed. This book is just one step on a long road of legitimization and legalization of psychedelics in mainstream "western" societies. Hopefully our societies will develop the wisdom and compassion to follow the evidence and weave these amazingly powerful medicines into the fabric of our society to allow for access to these healing and spiritual experiences.

Journey safely with an open and loving heart

Mark Haden

Appendix A

The following analogy can be used just before a participant ingests the medicine.

Canyon River Canoe Analogy

The purpose of this analogy is to provide a way of thinking about the psychedelic experience, to maximize the healing potential of these powerful medicines. The experience can take us to amazing places as we explore the wonderful complexity and depth of our own human experience. Important therapeutic work happens during the journey of self-exploration and healing.

It is helpful to know that the psychedelic experience opens many doors, and we can choose which parts of our experiences we are currently ready to explore. This is where proper preparation and an experienced guide comes in. The skill of working with psychedelic medicine is, in some ways, similar to the skill of paddling a canoe down a river flowing through a canyon.

> *On the river, you set out with companions. In your canoe there are people paddling with you who can help you get to where you want to go.*

The analogy with the psychedelic journey is that you are not alone. Experienced guides or therapists will be with you at all times so you can relax, knowing that your environment is safe, and that you will get the support you need from people who you can trust. Also, you can invite into your heart the people who have helped you along the way, until now, to join you on this journey.

> *On the river, when you push off your canoe from the shore, the banks gently rise beside you, guiding the direction of the journey. The banks are lush with trees,*

Manual for Psychedelic Guides

shrubs and grass. It takes great courage to embark on this voyage, and the many people who have gone before you often felt a little nervous at the start. This is okay. It means it matters. You have committed to the journey, and the river will now take you to your destination, where you can safely carry your canoe away from the flowing river.

The analogy with psychedelic medicine is that once you take the medication, you are also committed to the journey, and there is only one direction to go - down the river of time.

There are many factors that influence the experience of the canoe travelling down the river. One of them is the breeze, which can gently nudge you along or come upstream, asking you to meet its energy.

Within the psychedelic journey the environment of the experience is analogous to the breeze. The music, eyeshades and the setting of the room are all powerful and important parts of creating safety and a positive healing environment.

Another factor that influences the experience of canoeing in a canyon river is the fact that you have a paddle. It is not just the breeze which influences where you go, as you can paddle the canoe to the left or right of the river and move around obstacles on your journey.

You can make choices about where, in your mind, you focus your attention. You can pick and choose the parts of yourself you would like to explore. You can choose to stay in particular areas and to avoid others.

On a river, there are times when the water flows faster and becomes turbulent. You can be comforted by knowing

Mark Haden

that the guides are familiar with this river. There are life jackets to ensure everyone is safe and always above the water.

Within the psychedelic journey, the lifejacket is analogous to meditation, and staying focused on breathing. A skillful user of psychedelic medicines will practice taking long, slow, deep breaths and focusing on the sensations of breathing, to relax and induce a sense of calm. This allows their focus to remain on healing.

Many indigenous traditions believe that rivers have a spirit that can offer wisdom to someone who is able and willing to listen. We can learn from aboriginal people who have been using psychedelics or sacred medicines in healing ceremonies for centuries. Indigenous leaders who guide experiences with sacred plant medicines often advise that we approach the medicine with gratitude, and no matter what happens, to just say "thank you", to "trust the wisdom of the medicine" and to "trust your own Internal Healer". *Listening to the river is important when we paddle a canoe,* as is trusting the process when experiencing psychedelic medicine.

In preparation for your psychedelic healing journey, be aware that it is important to stay in the safety of the psychedelic treatment room. We will work with you to select music that supports your journey as it unfolds. It is also important to realize that you can pick and choose the issues that you would like to explore and bring into the healing experience. It will be important for you to practice slow deep breathing as this allows you to remain calm and relaxed during the experience. Remember, you will also have a guide with you at all times, to ensure your safety and to maximize the healing potential of the psychedelic experience. Finally, trust your own Internal Healer, trust the medicine, and no matter what happens, take a long slow deep breath and say, "thank you."

Manual for Psychedelic Guides

Mark Haden

Appendix B

Relaxing Meditation

This relaxing meditation begins with taking long slow deep breaths and breathing relaxation into different parts of the body. After this the guide describes how this experience may produce changes in perception, and to respond with, "Isn't this interesting..."! Colors may be more vivid, your body may feel different, your body may be bigger or smaller, you may see the music. The basic message for the session: trust the river, trust the journey, trust your own Internal Healer, trust in the wisdom of your own mind, trust in our relationship. Let go, be open. Let the music carry you. Trust the sacred medicine.

Interpersonal grounding: you'll never be alone during the period of drug-action. We're here with you. About hand holding and touching the shoulder - reach out any time (may demonstrate to normalize hand holding as comfortable energy flowing both ways, grounding). All emotions are welcome; anxiety, fear, laughter, tears, anger, awe, sexual feelings (can be felt but not expressed). Be yourself, open and honest. Allow these feelings to be experienced as a normal part of the journey – learn the lessons from the experience and allow the experience to change. Trust your own Internal Healer (the paddle allows you to explore where in the river you want to go as you flow down the river of personal exploration). Trust the sacred medicine, which will take you deep within, to a place beyond language, beyond thoughts, and then, of its own impetus, return you safely to the everyday world.

Manual for Psychedelic Guides

Appendix C

Music Suggestions:

	Musician	**CD/Album**
Beginning	Sarah Brightman	*Eden*
	R. Carlos Nakai	*Canyon Trilogy*
	Vangelis	*Antarctica*
	Vicki Hansen	*Earth Heart*
	Raphael	*Music to Disappear In*
	Kimba Arem	*Self-healing with Sound & Music*
	Peter Kater	*Resonance*
	Byron Metcalf	*Inner Rhythm Meditations*
Middle	Anugama	*Shamanic Dream 2*
	Anugama	*Sacred World*
	Kitaro	*Silk Road*
	Kitaro	*Tenku*
	Sacred Spirit	*Sacred Spirit 2*
	Kimba Arem	*Gaearth Dreaming*
	Sacred Spirit	*Chants & Dances of Native Americans*
	Culture clash	*Sacred Spirit Vol 2*
	Theda Phoenix	*Crystal Calm*
Ending	Jennifer Berezan	*Returning*
	Theda Phoenix	*Remergence*
	Dead can Dance	*Into the Labyrinth*
	Dead can Dance	*Toward the Within*
	Dead can Dance	*Spirit Chaser*
	Mythos	*Mythos*
	Tony O'Connor	*Uluru*
	Loreena Mckennit	*The Book of Secrets*
	John Serrie	*And the stars go with you*
	Between Interval	*Autumn Continent*
	Joanne Shenandoah	*Lifegivers*
	Andreas Vollenweider	*Trilogy*
	Louis Armstrong	*What a wonderful world*
	Beatles	*Here comes the sun*
	Beatles	*Lucy in the sky with Diamonds*

Mark Haden

Appendix D

Psychedelic Medicine Interactions with Pharmaceutical Medications: How to Analyze Possible Contraindications for Purposes of Safety

Dr. Trina Nguyen | BSc pharmacy, PharmD

This information is for educational purposes only. Please consult with your health care team for personalized medical advice

There is a growing body of evidence demonstrating efficacy for the use of psychedelics for PTSD, anxiety, depression, etc. Haphazardly, many who would benefit from these alternative remedies are concurrently prescribed pharmaceuticals that are listed in the literature, as contraindicated.

Gauging the risk of potential drug interactions can be a challenge. There is no formal reporting body to gather data (as there are for pharmaceuticals), and when an interaction is reported, there are multiple confounding factors such as set and setting (a significant factor for a favorable outcome), as well as unfortunate biases in the literature that lead readers to assume harm where it may not be substantiated by evidence.

The current standard of care takes a conservative approach with a full wash-out period of psychoactive medications. However, based on what we know of pharmacokinetics and pharmacodynamics, some medications may be taken concurrently, or, the window of effective wash-out can be shorter.

In the real world, many are adamant in going ahead with self-experimentation, and a facilitated set and setting is preferred over not having supervision. Being a facilitator, our first priority is safety. This document is to offer guidance on how to navigate when a client is taking concurrent chronic medications and would like to work with you.

Manual for Psychedelic Guides

Included below is a chart of pharmacodynamic interactions with psychoactive agents, which cross-references types of pharmaceutical medications with a selection of psychedelics. Beyond that is a description of practical and conservative approaches to pharmaceutical wash-out, including specific examples of SSRIs and MAOIs. Lastly, a chart of pharmacokinetic interactions illustrates additional considerations when combining pharmaceutical medications and psychedelic medicines.

The growing excitement around the effectiveness of these medicines to treat persistent mental health issues must be tempered by an understanding of pharmacological interactions with pharmaceutical medications currently being prescribed to a large portion of the population. Thankfully, with medicinal contraindication analysis, we can know whether there is legitimate basis for any concern and appropriate measures to be taken even in the cases where a contraindication is present. This practice will allow for the partnership between participant and practitioner to pursue a transformative experience while also ensuring set, setting, and safety.

Table 1: Pharmacodynamic interactions with psychoactive agents

Client's Therapy	Phenethylamines (MDMA, mescaline)	Tryptamines (psilocybin, LSD, DMT, 5-MEO-DMT)	Ayahuasca -contains MAOI
SSRI serotonin reuptake inhibitor ·citalopram (Celexa) ·fluoxetine (Prozac) ·paroxetine (Paxil) ·sertraline (Zoloft) **SNRI** serotonin norepinephrine reuptake inhibitor	Interaction: muted effect[3-5] SSRI/SNRI has higher affinity to receptor therefore blocking effect Approach may range from a short break in therapy to a full taper and wash-out	Interaction: muted effect[3] SSRI/SNRI has higher affinity to receptor therefore blocking effect Approach may range from a short break in therapy to a full	CONTRAINDICATED Interaction: risk of serotonin syndrome ranging from mild confusion to death[14] Clear from system for at least 2 weeks (fluoxetine longer)

Mark Haden

·Desvenlafaxine(Pristiq) ·Duloxetine (Cymbalta) ·Venlafaxine (Effexor)		taper and wash-out	
DNRI dopamine norepinephrine reuptake inhibitor ·bupropion (Wellbutrin)	MDMA Pharmacokinetic Interaction: increased subjective effects and longer duration[6]	No theoretical risk	Interaction: increased risk of side effects including hypertensive reactions[15]
TCA tricyclic antidepressant ·Amitriptyline (Elavil) ·Clomipramine (Anafranil) ·Desipramine (Norpramin) ·Imipramine (Tofranil) ·Nortriptyline (Pamelor)	Interaction: muted effect[1] TCA blocks serotonin receptor Approach may range from a short break in therapy to a full taper and wash-out	LSD interaction: increased subjective effects of LSD[9] Unknown interaction with other tryptamines but may range from muted effect to increased subjective effects Approach may range from a short break in therapy to a full taper and wash-out	Interaction: risk of serotonin syndrome with clomipramine and imipramine[16] Taper and clear clomipramine and imipramine from system for at least 2 weeks prior to therapy
MAO-A Inhibitors monoamine oxidase inhibitor ·Phenelzine (Nardil) ·Isocarboxazid (Parnate) ·Tranylcypromine (Marplan) ·Moclobemide ·Linezolid (Zyvox), antibiotic	CONTRAINDICATED Interaction: possible serotonin syndrome, hypertensive crisis and death[7,8] Taper and clear MAO-A from system for at least 2 weeks prior to therapy	5-MEO-DMT interaction: risk of serotonin syndrome[10] or increased effects and prolonged exposure[11] Taper and clear MAO-A from system for at least 2 weeks prior to therapy	Interaction: risk of serotonin syndrome and hypertensive episodes Taper and clear MAO-A from system for at least 2 weeks prior to therapy

Manual for Psychedelic Guides

		LSD interaction: may result in muted effect of LSD	
Lithium	Interaction: possible seizure; both MDMA and lithium decrease seizure threshold Clear lithium from system for at least 5 days prior to therapy	LSD interaction: Multiple reports of seizure and hospitalizations[2,1 3] LSD and psilocybin interaction: Increased effect of lithium Clear lithium from system for at least 5 days prior to therapy	Interaction: risk of serotonin syndrome Clear lithium from system for at least 5 days prior to therapy

Most Common Interaction - Muted Response

The most common interaction will be the muted response and the challenge to the sitter is to provide a consistent experience. The pharmacodynamics behind this response is due to:

- the serotonergic agonist (e.g. SSRI will bind with higher affinity to the serotonin receptor leaving the psychedelic unable to elucidate its effects)

- with consistent use, SSRIs down-regulate serotonin receptor activity limiting the amount of serotonin or psychedelic available for binding.

At this time, it is unknown which of these two mechanisms of action is more responsible for the muting of response, and additionally, each individual's brain chemistry differs. There is a both a flexible approach and a more conservative approach available to decrease the potential for a muted response.

Flexible Approach

The flexible approach is to discuss with your client their compliance history to identify if they've missed doses in the past and if they experienced any significant withdrawal symptoms. If withdrawal symptoms are manageable, discuss holding off on the medication, which would reduce the medication available in the synapse that competitively binds with the psychedelic. The hold window should allow for a decrease in the participant's medicine in their system by at least half (one half-life of the medicine). Pausing the medication for subsequent half-lives increases the chance of efficacy for the psychedelic, though this should be balanced against the effects of not taking the medication.

Example:

Paroxetine (Paxil) half-life is 21 hours. If paroxetine is held for 21 hours, there will be 50% less of the medication available to block the psychedelic. A potential course of action is to ask the patient to hold the day's dose before the journey as well as the morning dose the day of the journey (at least 21 hours). Holding for additional half-lives (i.e. 42-63 hours) will increase the possibility that the participant feels the effect of the psychedelic. Paroxetine may be taken once the psychedelic effect has worn away.

Conservative Approach

If a conservative approach of a taper and wash-out period is more comfortable, the sitter may work with the client's health care professional and follow the protocol designed and employed by MAPS for their trials. In the trial, the investigators tapered as per an individualized plan, then held for at least five times the particular drug and active metabolites' half-life, plus one week for stabilization in order to return to your body's natural baseline.

Manual for Psychedelic Guides

Example:

Bupropion (Wellbutrin) half-life is 21 hours. Because of the serious risk of combining bupropion with an MAOI, a full wash-out period of 5 half-lives ensures that all of the medication in the participant's system has been cleared. Following the MAPS protocol, a tapering schedule is applied that was devised with the client's health care professional, then a wash-out period of 5 days followed by 7 days for stabilization. Bupropion may be restarted once the MAOI has fully cleared from the body.

Table 2: MAPS Prescription Medication Tapering Table

Generic Name	Brand Name	Half-life (hours) Including Active Metabolites	Days for Washout
alprazolam	Xanax	11	3
aripiprazole	Abilify	75	16
atomoxetine	Strattera	5-24	5
bupropion	Wellbutrin	21	5
citalopram	Celexa	35	8
clonazepam	Klonopin	30-40	8
diazepam	Valium	20-70	15
duloxetine	Cymbalta	12	3
escitalopram	Lexapro	32	7
fluoxetine	Prozac	7-9 days	45
imiprimine	Tofranil	6-18	4
lamotrigine	Lamictal	25	6
lorazepam	Ativan	12	3
mirtazapine	Remeron	20-40	8
olanzapine	Zyprexa	21-54	11
paroxetine	Paxil	21	5
prazosin	Minipress	2-3	1
quetiapine	Seroquel	6	2
risperidone	Risperdal	3-20	4

sertraline	Zoloft	26	6
temazepam	Restoril	8-12	3
trazodone	Desyrel	9	2
venlafaxine	Effexor	12	3
ziprasidone	Geodon	7	2
zolpidem	Ambien	2.5	<1

source: https://maps.org/research-archive/mdma/MP12_FINAL_Protocol_Amendment_5_Version_1_19Aug14_web.pdf

Potential Serious Interaction - Serotonin Syndrome

Also known as serotonin toxicity, serotonin syndrome results from excess serotonin in the brain synapses from drugs that are serotonergically active. Serotonin syndrome symptoms may range from mild, non-specific adverse events such as confusion, agitation or restlessness, headache, nausea, vomiting, sweating and shivering, to more concerning events such as tremor, loss of muscle coordination or twitching, rapid heart rate and can be potentially fatal. Caution is often cited in the resources that SSRIs combined with either MDMA or tryptamines leads to serotonin syndrome. In theory, this interaction exists. However, with further understanding of pharmacodynamics the above interaction of muted response explains why the concern is pacified.

Potential Serious Interaction - Pharmacokinetic Interactions

In addition to pharmacodynamic interactions, there are also pharmacokinetic interactions. The liver uses enzymes, known as the CYP450 system to metabolize and breakdown compounds in the bloodstream. When we intake psychedelics, pharmaceuticals, herbals, and even food, often times we are activating this system to safely clear the chemicals from our bodies. When there is competition between a psychedelic and another molecule on the same enzyme, the pharmacokinetic effect can be an increase in the psychedelic in the blood, potentially leading to an accidental overdose. Unfortunately, this interaction is difficult to predict as

Manual for Psychedelic Guides

serum drug concentrations do not necessarily correlate with subjective or toxic effects of the psychedelic. In other words, even if the psychedelic concentration is raised in the bloodstream, the psychedelic still needs to enter the central nervous system to elucidate an effect, which is tightly controlled by the blood-brain-barrier.

Table 3: Hepatic Metabolism of Selected Psychedelics (illustrative, not comprehensive)

psychedelic	Parent molecule activity	Metabolized by Enzyme	Metabolite	Active/Inactive
MDMA	active	CYP2D6	DHMA	inactive
Ibogaine	active	CYP2D6	noribogaine	active
5-MEO-DMT	active	CYP2D6	bufotenine	minor active
LSD	active	multiple CYP450 enzymes	numerous metabolites	inactive

Referencing the above table, the enzyme CYP2D6 is responsible for the breakdown of MDMA, ibogaine, and 5-MEO-DMT. Inhibition of the CYP2D6 enzyme will result in increased levels in the blood and potential increased duration of effect. Examples of strong pharmaceutical inhibitors of the CYP2D6 enzyme include paroxetine, bupropion, quinidine, cinacalcet, and fluoxetine. LSD inhibition is not a concern as it is broken down by multiple enzymes.

As mentioned previously, an increase in plasma levels do not necessarily equate to an increase in subjective effects or toxicity.

Mark Haden

Study 1: Fatal case report of MDMA with ritonavir

MDMA in combination with ritonavir (protease inhibitor and potent 2D6 inhibitor) resulted in an increase of over 10-fold levels in blood upon autopsy. (Antoniou, 2002)

Study 2: Case report of MDMA with fluoxetine

MDMA in combination with fluoxetine (strong 2D6 inhibitor) resulted in a muted response.

Explanation: despite a likely increase in plasma levels, there is a competing pharmacodynamic interaction *decreases* available MDMA to the site of action negating this interaction *see pharmacodynamic interactions table for guidance*

Study 3: Trial of ibogaine with paroxetine

A study using paroxetine as a strong CYP2D6 inhibitor demonstrated ibogaine-noribogaine exposure increased by approximately 2-fold (Glue, 2015)

As demonstrated by the studies above, it is important to identify if there is competition in the metabolism of the psychedelic, but there are additional factors that must be considered before changing therapy. If you want to perform the most rigorous analysis, you may cross-reference enzymes metabolized by your client's current medications to the enzymes impacted by the psychedelic they are considering taking. Whenever there is a conflict, it is important to consider the potentially amplifying effects in the liver and provide informed consent to any potential participants whose medications may be contraindicated.

Manual for Psychedelic Guides

Source Acknowledgment

This document was created using 3 foundational documents:

1) Guide Manual by Karen Cooper (Usona, v2014))

2) A Manual for MDMA-Assisted Psychotherapy in the Treatment of Posttraumatic Stress Disorder by Michael Mitheofer (v2015)

3) Developing Guidelines and Competencies for the Training of Psychedelic Guides by Janis Phelps (2017)

Suggested Reading

Abramson, H. A. (Ed.) (1967). *The use of LSD in psychotherapy and alcoholism.* Indianapolis:Bobbs-Merrill.

Ball, M. W. (2017). *Entheogenic Liberation: Unraveling the Enigma of Nonduality with 5-MeO-DMT Energetic Therapy.* Ashland Oregon: Kyandara Publishing.

Blewett, D. B., & Chwelos, N. (1959). *Handbook for the Therapeutic Use of Lysergic Acid Diethylamine-25: Individual and Group Procedures.*

Carhart-Harris, R. L., Leech, R., Hellyer, , P. J., S., M., Feilding, A., Tagliazucchi, E., & Nutt, D. (2014). The entropic brain: A theory of conscious states informed by neuroimaging research with psychedelic drugs. *Frontiers in Human Neuroscience, 8*(20), 1-22. doi:doi:10.3389/fnhum.2014.00020

Coleman, R. (2017). *Psychedelic Psychotherapy: A user friendly guide to psychedelic drug assisted psychotherapy.* Berkley, CA: Transform Press.

Code of Ethics for Spiritual Guides. Retrieved from http://www.csp.org/code.html

Mark Haden

Cooper, K. (2014). *Guide Manual for pharmacokinetics of psilocybin in healthy adult volunteers study.* University of Wisconsin, Madison: Usona.

Fadiman, J. (2011). *The Psychedelic Explorers Guide: Safe, therapeutic and sacred journeys.* Rochester, VT: Park Street Press.

Fischer, F. M. (2015). *Therapy with substance: Psycholytic psychotherapy in the twenty first century.* London, New York: Muswell Hill Press.

Garcia-Romeu, A., Griffiths, R. R., & Johnson, M. W. (2014). Psilocybin-occasioned mystical experiences in the treatment of tobacco addiction. *Current drug abuse reviews, 7*(3), 157-164.

Greer, G. R., & Tolbert, R. (1998). A method of conducting therapeutic sessions with MDMA. *J Psychoactive Drugs, 30*(4), 371-379. doi:10.1080/02791072.1998.10399713

Griffiths, R., Richards, W., Johnson, M., McCann, U., & Jesse, R. (2008). Mystical-type experiences occasioned by psilocybin mediate the attribution of personal meaning and spiritual significance 14 months later. *Journal of Psychopharmacology., 22*(6), 621-632. doi:10.1177/0269881108094300

Griffiths, R. R., Johnson, M. W., Carducci, M. A., Umbricht, A., Richards, W. A., Richards, B. D., . . . Klinedinst, M. A. (2016). Psilocybin produces substantial and sustained decreases in depression and anxiety in patients with life-threatening cancer: A randomized double-blind trial. *Journal of psychopharmacology, 30*(12), 1181-1197. doi:10.1177/0269881116675513

Griffiths, R. R., Johnson, M. W., Richards, W. A., Richards, B. D., McCann, U., & Jesse, R. (2011). Psilocybin occasioned mystical-type experiences: immediate and persisting dose-related effects. *Psychopharmacology (Berl), 218*(4), 649-665. doi:10.1007/s00213-011-2358-5

Griffiths, R. R., Richards, W. A., McCann, U., & Jesse, R. (2006). Psilocybin can occasion mystical-type experiences having substantial and sustained personal meaning and spiritual significance.

Psychopharmacology (Berl), 187(3), 268-283; discussion 284-292. doi:10.1007/s00213-006-0457-5

Grof, S. (2001). *LSD Psychotherapy* (Forth edition ed.). Santa Cruz, CA, USA.: Multidisciplinary Association for Psychedelic Studies.

Johnson, M., Richards, W., & Griffiths, R. (2008). Human hallucinogen research: guidelines for safety. *Journal of psychopharmacology, 22*(6), 603-620. doi:10.1177/0269881108093587

Johnson, M. W., Garcia-Romeu, A., & Griffiths, R. R. (2017). Long-term follow-up of psilocybin-facilitated smoking cessation. *The American journal of drug and alcohol abuse, 43*(1), 55-60. doi:10.3109/00952990.2016.1170135

Johnson, M. W., & Griffiths, R. R. (2017). Potential Therapeutic Effects of Psilocybin. *Neurotherapeutics.* doi:10.1007/s13311-017-0542-y

MacLean, K. A., Johnson, M. W., & Griffiths, R. R. (2011). Mystical experiences occasioned by the hallucinogen psilocybin lead to increases in the personality domain of openness. *Journal of Psychopharmacology., 25*(11), 1453-1461. doi:10.1177/0269881111420188

Metzner, R. (2015). *Allies for Awakening: Guidelines for productive and safe experiences with entheogens.* Berkley California: Regent Press.

Miller, J. *The Art of Being a Healing Presence.*

Miller, J. E., & Cutshall, S. C. (2001). *The Art of Being a Healing Presence: A guide for those in caring relationships.* Fort Wayne, Indiana: Willowgreen Publisher.

Mithoefer, M. C. (2013). *A Manual for MDMA-Assisted Psychotherapy in the Treatment of Posttraumatic Stress Disorder.* Retrieved from Santa Cruz, CA:

Passie, T. (2009). *Healing with Entactogens: Guide and Patient Perspectives on MDMA-Assisted Group Psychotherapy* Santa Cruz, CA: Multidisciplinary Association for Psychedelic Studies.

Phelps, J. (2017). Developing Guidelines and Competencies for the Training of Psychedelic Guides. *Journal of Humanistic Psychology, 57*(5), 450-487.

Stolaroff, M. J. (1997). *The Secret Chief: Conversations with a Pioneer of the Underground Psychedelic Therapy Movement.* Charlotte, N.C.: Multidisciplinary Association for Psychedelic Studies (MAPS).

Taylor, K. (1995). *The Ethics of Caring: Honoring the web of life in our professional healing relationships.* Santa Cruz, California: Handford Mead Publishers.

Manual for Psychedelic Guides

References - main text

1. Andritzky, W., *Sociopsychotherapeutic functions of ayahuasca healing in Amazonia.* Journal of Psychoactive Drugs, 1989. **21**(1): p. 77-89.
2. McKenna, D.J., *Ayahuasca: An ethnopharmacologic history*, in *Ayahuasca: Hallucinogens, consciousness, and the spirit of nature*, R. Metzner, Editor. 1999, Thunder's Mouth Press: New York. p. 187-213.
3. Labate, B.C., I.S.d. Rose, and R.G.d. Santos, eds. *Ayahuasca Religions: A Comprehensive Bibliography and Critical Essays*. 2008, MAPS: Santa Cruz, CA.
4. Heaven, R. and H.G. Charing, *Plant Spirit Shamanism*. 2006, Rochester, Vermont: Destiny.
5. Stewart, O., C, *Peyote Religion*. 1987, Norman: University of Oklahoma Press.
6. Smith, H. and R. Snake, eds. *One nation under god: The triumph of the Native American church*. 1996, Clear Light Publishers: Santa Fe, NM.
7. Labate, B.C. and C. Cavnar, *Peyote: History, Tradition, Politics and Conservation*. 2016, Santa Barbara, CA: Praeger.
8. Fernandez, J.W. and R.L. Fernandez, *Returning to the path: The use of ibogaine in a equatorial African Ritual Context and the binding of time, space and social relationships*, in *The Alkaloids,*. 2001, Academic Press, Department of Anthropology the University of Chicago: Chicago. p. 235-247.
9. Dobkin de Rios, M., *The wilderness of mind: Sacred plants in cross-cultural perspective*. Sage research papers in the social sciences (Cross-cultural studies series, No. 90-027). 1976, London: Sage Publications.
10. Dobkin de Rios, M., *Visonary Vine, Hallucinogenic healing in the Peruvian Amazon*. 1972, Long Grove: Waveland Press.
11. Dobkin de Rios, M., *Hallucinogens: Cross-cultural perspectives*. 1984, Albequerque, NM: University of New Mexico Press.
12. Dyck, E., *Psychedelic psychiatry: LSD from clinic to campus*. 2008, Baltimore, MD: Johns Hopkins University Press.

13. Griffiths, R.R., et al., *Psilocybin produces substantial and sustained decreases in depression and anxiety in patients with life-threatening cancer: A randomized double-blind trial.* Journal of Psychopharmacology, 2016. **30**(12): p. 1181-1197.
14. Dos Santos, R.G., et al., *Antidepressive, anxiolytic, and antiaddictive effects of ayahuasca, psilocybin and lysergic acid diethylamide (LSD): a systematic review of clinical trials published in the last 25 years.* Theraputic Advances in Psychopharmacology, 2016. **6**(3): p. 193-213.
15. Johnson, M.W., et al., *Pilot study of the 5-HT2AR agonist psilocybin in the treatment of tobacco addiction.* Journal of Psychopharmacology, 2014. **28**(11): p. 983-992.
16. Krebs, T.S. and P.O. Johansen, *Lysergic acid diethylamide (LSD) for alcoholism: meta-analysis of randomized controlled trials.* Journal of Psychopharmacology., 2012. **26**(7): p. 994-1002.
17. Sewell, R.A., J.H. Halpern, and H.G. Pope, Jr., *Response of cluster headache to psilocybin and LSD.* Neurology, 2006. **66**(12): p. 1920-1922.
18. Mithoefer, M.C., et al., *3,4-methylenedioxymethamphetamine (MDMA)-assisted psychotherapy for post-traumatic stress disorder in military veterans, firefighters, and police officers: a randomised, double-blind, dose-response, phase 2 clinical trial.* Lancet Psychiatry, 2018. **5**(6): p. 486-497.
19. Mithoefer, M.C., et al., *The safety and efficacy of 3, 4-methylenedioxymethamphetamine-assisted psychotherapy in subjects with chronic, treatment-resistant posttraumatic stress disorder: the first randomized controlled pilot study.* Journal of Psychopharmacology., 2010. **25**(4): p. 439-52.
20. Mithoefer, M.C., et al., *Durability of improvement in post-traumatic stress disorder symptoms and absence of harmful effects or drug dependency after 3,4-methylenedioxymethamphetamine-assisted psychotherapy: a prospective long-term follow-up study.* Journal of Psychopharmacology, 2013. **27**(1): p. 28-39.

21. Moreno, F.A., et al., *Safety, tolerability, and efficacy of psilocybin in 9 patients with obsessive-compulsive disorder.* Journal of Clinical Psychiatry, 2006. **67**(11): p. 1735-1740.
22. Whelan, A. and M.I. Johnson, *Lysergic acid diethylamide and psilocybin for the management of patients with persistent pain: a potential role?* Pain Manag, 2018. **8**(3): p. 217-229.
23. Walsh, Z., et al., *Hallucinogen use and intimate partner violence: Prospective evidence consistent with protective effects among men with histories of problematic substance use.* J Psychopharmacol, 2016. **30**(7): p. 601-607.
24. Hendricks, P.S., et al., *Hallucinogen use predicts reduced recidivism among substance-involved offenders under community corrections supervision.* Journal of Psychopharmacology, 2014. **28**(1): p. 62-66.
25. Hendricks, P.S., et al., *Classic psychedelic use is associated with reduced psychological distress and suicidality in the United States adult population.* Journal of Psychopharmacology, 2015. **29**(3): p. 280-288.
26. Argento, E., et al., *The moderating effect of psychedelics on the prospective relationship between prescription opioid use and suicide risk among marginalized women.* J Psychopharmacol, 2018. **32**(12): p. 1385-1391.
27. Forstmann, M., et al., *Transformative experience and social connectedness mediate the mood-enhancing effects of psychedelic use in naturalistic settings.* Proc Natl Acad Sci U S A, 2020. **117**(5): p. 2338-2346.
28. Carhart-Harris, R.L., et al., *Psychedelics and connectedness.* Psychopharmacology (Berl), 2018. **235**(2): p. 547-550.
29. Kettner, H., et al., *From Egoism to Ecoism: Psychedelics Increase Nature Relatedness in a State-Mediated and Context-Dependent Manner.* Int J Environ Res Public Health, 2019. **16**(24).
30. Amoroso, T. and M. Workman, *Treating posttraumatic stress disorder with MDMA-assisted psychotherapy: A preliminary meta-analysis and comparison to prolonged exposure therapy.* J Psychopharmacol, 2016. **30**(7): p. 595-600.

31. Dos Santos, R.G., et al., *Classical hallucinogens and neuroimaging: A systematic review of human studies: Hallucinogens and neuroimaging.* Neurosci Biobehav Rev, 2016. **71**: p. 715-728.
32. Passie, T., et al., *The pharmacology of lysergic acid diethylamide: a review.* CNS Neurosci Ther, 2008. **14**(4): p. 295-314.
33. Dos Santos, R.G., et al., *The current state of research on ayahuasca: A systematic review of human studies assessing psychiatric symptoms, neuropsychological functioning, and neuroimaging.* J Psychopharmacol, 2016.
34. Dos Santos, R.G., et al., *Efficacy, tolerability, and safety of serotonergic psychedelics for the management of mood, anxiety, and substance-use disorders: a systematic review of systematic reviews.* Expert Review of Clinical Pharmacology, 2018.
35. Nunes, A.A., et al., *Effects of Ayahuasca and its Alkaloids on Drug Dependence: A Systematic Literature Review of Quantitative Studies in Animals and Humans.* J Psychoactive Drugs, 2016. **48**(3): p. 195-205.
36. Mangini, M., *Treatment of alcoholism using psychedelic drugs: a review of the program of research.* J Psychoactive Drugs, 1998. **30**(4): p. 381-418.
37. Dos Santos, R.G. and J.E.C. Hallak, *Therapeutic use of serotoninergic hallucinogens: A review of the evidence and of the biological and psychological mechanisms.* Neurosci Biobehav Rev, 2019. **108**: p. 423-434.
38. Griffiths, R.R., et al., *Psilocybin can occasion mystical-type experiences having substantial and sustained personal meaning and spiritual significance.* Psychopharmacology (Berl), 2006. **187**(3): p. 268-83; discussion 284-92.
39. Griffiths, R.R., et al., *Psilocybin occasioned mystical-type experiences: immediate and persisting dose-related effects.* Psychopharmacology (Berl), 2011. **218**(4): p. 649-65.
40. Johnson, M.W., et al., *The abuse potential of medical psilocybin according to the 8 factors of the Controlled Substances Act.* Neuropharmacology, 2018. **142**: p. 143-166.

Manual for Psychedelic Guides

41. Nutt, D., et al., *Development of a rational scale to assess the harm of drugs of potential misuse.* Lancet, 2007. **369**(9566): p. 1047-53.
42. Nutt, D.J., et al., *Drug harms in the UK: a multicriteria decision analysis.* Lancet, 2010. **376**(9752): p. 1558-1565.
43. van Amsterdam, J., A. Opperhuizen, and W. van den Brink, *Harm potential of magic mushroom use: a review.* Regul Toxicol Pharmacol, 2011. **59**(3): p. 423-9.
44. EMCDDA -European Monitoring Centre for Drugs and Drug Addiction, *Hallucinogenic mushrooms: An emerging trend case study.* 2006.
45. Tupper, K.W., et al., *Psychedelic medicine: a re-emerging therapeutic paradigm.* Canadian Medical Association Journal, 2015. **187**(14): p. 1054-1059.
46. Metzner, R., *Allies for awakening: Guidelines for productive and safe experiences with entheogens.* 2015, Berkley California: Regent Press.
47. Bache, C., *LSD and the mind of the Universe: Diamonds from heaven.* 2019, Rochester Vermont: Park Street Press.
48. Phelps, J., *Developing Guidelines and Competencies for the Training of Psychedelic Therapists.* Journal of Humanistic Psychology, 2017. **57**(5): p. 450-487.
49. Earp, B.D. and J. Savulescu, *Love Drugs: The Chemical Future of Relationships.* 2020, Stanford, California: Redwood Press.

Appendix D – Drug Interactions References:

1. Bronson, Kit. "The Interactions between Hallucinogens and Antidepressants" Erowid.org, 3 October 1994, Erowid.org/chemicals/maois/maois_info4.shtml
2. Malcolm BJ. *Antidepressants and 3,4-methylenedioxymethamphetamine (MDMA): Blunted Experiences & Mechanisms of Drug Interaction.* Poster presented at the Los Angeles Psychedelic Science Symposium 2018: June 22nd; Los Angeles CA

3. Farre, M., et al., Pharmacological interaction between 3,4-methylenedioxymethamphetamine (ecstasy) and paroxetine: pharmacological effects and pharmacokinetics. J Pharmacol Exp Ther, 2007. 323(3): p. 954-62.
4. Stein, D.J. and J. Rink, Effects of "Ecstasy" blocked by serotonin reuptake inhibitors. J Clin Psychiatry, 1999. 60(7): p. 485.
5. Hysek, C.M., et al., Duloxetine inhibits effects of MDMA ("ecstasy") in vitro and in humans in a randomized placebo-controlled laboratory study. PLoS One, 2012. 7(5): p. E36476.
6. Schmid, Y., et al., Interactions between bupropion and 3,4-methylenedioxymethamphetamine in healthy subjects. J Pharmacol Exp Ther, 2015. 353(1): p. 102-11.
7. Vuori E, Henry J Ojanpera I, Nieminen R, Savolainen T, Wahlsten P et al. Death following ingestion of MDMA (ecstasy) and moclobemide. Addiction 2003;98(3):365-8.
8. Kaskey G. Possible interaction between an MAOI and ecstasy. Am J of Psychiatry 1992;149:411-2.
9. Bonson KR, Murphy DL. "Alterations in responses to LSD in humans associated with chronic administration of tricyclic antidepressants, monoamine oxidase inhibitors or lithium". Behav Brain Res. 1996 Dec; 73(1-2):229-33.
10. Brush DE, Bird SB, Boyer EW. "Monoamine oxidase inhibitor poisoning resulting from Internet misinformation on illicit substances." J Toxicol Clin Toxicol. 2004 Jun;42(2):191-5.
11. Shen, H. W., Jiang, X. L., Winter, J. C., & Yu, A. (2010). Psychedelic 5-methoxy-N,N-dimethyltryptamine: Metabolism, pharmacokinetics, drug interactions, and pharmacological actions. Current Drug Metabolism, 11(8), 659-66.
12. Fisher D, Ungerleider J. "Grand mal seizures following ingestion of LSD." Calif Med. 1967 Mar; 106(3): 210–11.
13. Brown M. "Interactions Between LSD and Antidepressants". Erowid.org. Oct 16 2003. Erowid.org/chemicals/lsd/lsd_health3.shtml

Manual for Psychedelic Guides

14. Erowid. "Interactions Between MAOIs, SSRIs, and Recreational Drugs." Erowid.org. 14 January 2020. Erowid.org/chemicals/maois/maois_info8.shtml
15. RXList. "Wellbutrin" RXList.com. 14 January 2020. Rxlist.com/wellbutrin-drug.htm#side_effects
16. Gilman, K., Monoamine oxidase inhibitors: A review concerning dietary tyramine and drug interactions. PsychoTropical Commentaries, 2017. 1(1): p. 105
17. Antoniou T, Tseng AL-i (2002) Interactions between recreational drugs and antiretroviral agents. Ann Pharmacother 36(10):1598–1613
18. Glue P, Winter H. "Influence of CYP2D6 activity on the pharmacokinetics and pharmacodynamics of a single 20 mg dose of ibogaine in healthy volunteers". The Journal of Clinical Pharmacology. 2015;55(6):680-87

Manufactured by Amazon.ca
Bolton, ON